Retirement Ready: 40+ Low-Budget Business Ideas for Financial Independence

By Grace Campbell

Easy Reads Publishing
2024

Contents

1. Key Making Services 6
2. Wooden Cases 9
3. Manicure Printer 13
4. Power Bank Vending Machines 16
5. Laser Engraving Machine 21
6. Badge Making Machine 25
7. Engraver Pen 30
8. Drones for Video Shooting 34
9. Hydroponic Farming Kits 38
10. Subscription Box Service 43
11. DIY Candle Making Kits 47
12. Personalized Phone Cases 52
13. Handmade Soap Production 55
14. Vertical Garden Kits 60
15. Aquaponics Systems 63
16. Digital Marketing Consultancy 67
17. Remote Tech Support 71
18. Virtual Event Planning 76
19. E-book Publishing 80
20. Language Translation Services 83
21. Online Tutoring 87
22. Virtual Fitness Coaching 91
23. Podcast Production Services 96

24. Mobile Car Wash 100
25. Pet Grooming 105
26. House Cleaning 110
27. Gardening Services 114
28. Interior Design Consultancy 119
29. Home Staging 123
30. Personal Styling 128
31. Professional Organizing 128
32. Event Photography 133
33. Portrait Photography 138
34. Product Photography 143
35. Real Estate Photography 149
36. Videography Services 154
37. Drone Photography 159
38. Digital Illustration 165
39. Graphic Design 170
40. Web Design 176
41. Social Media Management 182
42. Content Writing 183
43. Copyediting and Proofreading 185
44. Resume Writing 185
45. Virtual Assistant 188
46. Life Coaching 191
Your Next Step: Turning Ideas into Reality 195

Disclaimer

The ideas, examples, and resources provided in this book are intended for informational and inspirational purposes only. While we strive to offer valuable insights and suggestions, there is no guarantee of income, success, or specific results from implementing the concepts discussed herein. Business ventures are inherently risky, and outcomes can vary widely based on numerous factors including market conditions, individual effort, and business acumen.

The examples and resources included are meant to illustrate potential approaches and should not be construed as definitive solutions or guarantees of success. Each business situation is unique, and it is crucial for you to conduct thorough research, seek professional advice, and invest your own time and effort to tailor strategies to your specific circumstances.

Your active involvement, dedication, and hard work are critical components of any business endeavor. We encourage you to use the ideas presented as a starting point and adapt them to fit your personal goals and objectives.

We wish you success in your entrepreneurial journey and remind you that the ultimate responsibility for your business decisions rests with you.

Hey there, future entrepreneur! If you're reading this, you're probably thinking about starting a business in your retirement years. Well, you've come to the right place!

Let's get one thing straight right off the bat: this book isn't a magic wand that'll turn you into an overnight millionaire. (Wouldn't that be nice, though?) Instead, think of it as your friendly guide, packed with ideas, examples, and resources to inspire you on your entrepreneurial journey.

Now, you might be thinking, "Starting a business? At my age? That sounds expensive!" But here's the thing – it doesn't have to be. We're going to show you how to launch a business on a shoestring budget. Whether you're looking for a fun side hustle or dreaming of a full-blown second career, we've got you covered.

One of the keys to success? Marketing. Don't worry, we're not talking about flashy TV commercials or expensive billboards. We'll explore plenty of budget-friendly ways to get the word out about your new venture.

Of course, every business needs some basic tools to keep things running smoothly. We'll chat about affordable options for accounting and customer management – and hey, sometimes a simple Excel spreadsheet is all you need to get started!

Now, let's talk about something that might not be the most exciting topic, but it's super important:

insurance. I know, I know, it sounds like a snooze-fest. But trust me, protecting your new business is crucial, especially when you're in retirement. We'll break down the types of insurance you might need, from general liability to cyber protection.

Here's the best part: this book is packed with over 40 business ideas that you can start without breaking the bank. Whether you're a tech whiz, a crafting genius, or a people person, there's something in here for you.

Remember, retirement isn't about slowing down – it's about having the freedom to chase your dreams. Starting a business can be a fantastic way to stay active, earn some extra cash, and maybe even leave a lasting legacy.

So, are you ready to embark on this exciting new chapter? Grab a cup of coffee (or tea, if that's more your style), get comfy, and let's dive in. Your next great adventure is waiting!

1. Key Making Services

Investing in key-making equipment enables entrepreneurs to offer key duplication and customization services to hotels, businesses, and individuals, tapping into a steady market demand.

Here's what you'll need to get started:

1. Skills and Training

- Key Cutting Skills: Basic training in key cutting is essential. You can learn through online courses, apprenticeships, or by working with an experienced locksmith.
- Locksmithing Knowledge: Understanding the different types of keys and locks is important. You might need to know how to handle key blanks, key machines, and the different cuts required for different locks.

2. Equipment and Tools

- Key Cutting Machine: This is the primary tool for making keys. There are various types, such as manual, semi-automatic, and automatic key cutting machines.
- Key Blanks: A stock of key blanks is essential. These are uncut keys that can be shaped according to the lock pattern.
- Calipers and Gauges: These tools help in measuring the depth and spacing of key cuts to ensure accuracy.
- Duplicator Machine: Used for copying existing keys.
- Laser Key Cutting Machine (Optional): If you plan to cut high-security or automotive keys.

3. Supplies

- Lubricants: For maintaining the key-cutting machines.
- Brushes: To clean the machines and work area.

- Safety Gear: Such as goggles, gloves, and ear protection.

4. Licenses and Permits

- Business License: You'll need to register your business with the local authorities.
- Locksmith License: Depending on your location, you may need a special locksmith license or certification.
- Insurance: General liability insurance to protect against any potential damage claims.

5. Location

- Physical Storefront: If you plan to operate a traditional store, choose a location with good foot traffic.
- Mobile Service: A van equipped with key-making equipment for on-the-go services.

6. Marketing

- Signage: Clear, visible signs to attract customers.
- Online Presence: A website or social media presence can help attract more customers.
- Local Advertising: Flyers, business cards, or ads in local directories.

7. Business Management

- Pricing Strategy: Competitive pricing based on the market and your operating costs.

- Customer Service: A friendly and professional approach to ensure repeat customers.
- Record Keeping: Keep accurate records of sales, expenses, and inventory.

Starting with these essentials will set a strong foundation for your key-making service.

2. Wooden Cases

Crafting wooden cases or computer cases appeal to tech enthusiasts seeking unique and aesthetically pleasing hardware solutions. Birch plywood and other wood varieties offer durability and visual appeal, making them popular choices for custom builds.

Starting a wooden case business involves a mix of woodworking and electronics knowledge. Here's a detailed list of tools and equipment you'll need to get started:

1. Equipment and Tools
   a. **Sawing Tools:**
   - Table Saw: Essential for making precise cuts on large pieces of wood.
   - Miter Saw Useful for making angled cuts and crosscuts.
   - Circular Saw: Handy for cutting larger sheets of wood or making rough cuts.
   - Jigsaw: Ideal for making intricate cuts and curves.

   b. **Cutting Tools:**
   - Router: For creating decorative edges, grooves, and slots in wood.
   - Drill: For drilling holes and creating mounting points. A drill press can also be useful for precision.

c. **Sanding Tools**:
   - Orbital Sander: For smoothing large surfaces and removing roughness.
   - Detail Sander: For smaller, intricate areas where an orbital sander might be too large.

d. **Joinery Tools:**
   - Clamps: Various sizes for holding pieces together while gluing or assembling.
   - Wood Glue: High-quality adhesive for wood joints.
   - Screws and Fasteners: To assemble and secure different parts of the case.

e. **Measuring and Marking Tools**:
   - Tape Measure: For accurate measurements.
   - Square: For ensuring right angles.
   - Calipers: For precise measurements of components and fittings.
   - Marking Tools: Pencils, marking gauges, or chalk for marking cut lines and measurements.

2. **Computer Case Specific Tools**

   a. Ventilation and Cooling Solutions:
   - Drill Bits: For creating holes for cooling fans and ventilation.
   - Grills and Mesh: For covering ventilation holes and improving airflow.

b. **Hardware Mounting Tools:**
   - Screwdriver Set: A variety of screwdrivers, including Phillips and flathead, for assembling and mounting hardware.
   - Threaded Inserts: For mounting components like motherboards, power supplies, and drives.

3. Finishing Tools

   a. Paint and Finishes:
   - Paint Sprayer or Brushes: For applying paint or varnish to the wooden case.
   - Wood Stain: To enhance the natural look of the wood.
   - Varnish or Polyurethane: For protecting the wood surface and adding a glossy finish.

   b. Sandpaper: Various grits for smoothing and preparing surfaces before finishing.

4. Safety Equipment

   a. Personal Protective Equipment (PPE):
   - Safety Glasses: To protect your eyes from sawdust and debris.
   - Dust Mask: To prevent inhaling fine dust particles.
   - Hearing Protection: Earplugs or earmuffs to protect your hearing from loud machinery.

   b. First Aid Kit: For addressing any minor injuries or accidents.

5. Assembly and Testing Tools

   a. Computer Assembly Tools:
   - Anti-Static Wrist Strap: To prevent static damage to electronic components.
   - Cable Management Supplies: Cable ties, clips, and sleeves for organizing internal cables.

   b. Testing Equipment:
   - Thermal Sensors or Temperature Gauges: To monitor the internal temperature of the computer case.
   - Fan Controllers: For managing airflow and cooling within the case.

6. Workshop Setup

   a. Workbench - A sturdy workbench with ample space for cutting, assembling, and finishing.
   b. Storage Solutions Shelving and Tool Racks for organizing and storing tools, materials, and finished products.
   c. Ventilation:
   d. Proper ventilation in your workspace to manage dust and fumes from wood finishing products.

7. Miscellaneous Tools

   a. Adhesives and Sealants
   - Wood Filler: For filling any gaps or imperfections in the wood.
   - Sealant: To protect wood from moisture and enhance durability.

b. **Computer Hardware Components:** Such as motherboards, power supplies, and drives to ensure compatibility and test fit.

By equipping yourself with these tools and setting up an efficient workspace, you'll be well-prepared to start your wooden computer case business. Focus on precision and craftsmanship to create high-quality, attractive cases that appeal to your target market.

3. Manicure Printer

Compact and user-friendly manicure printers revolutionize nail art, allowing individuals to create intricate designs effortlessly. These devices cater to both professionals and DIY enthusiasts, offering versatility and convenience.

Starting a manicure printer business involves both understanding the technology behind nail art printing and having the right tools and equipment to produce high-quality designs. Here's a comprehensive list of the tools and equipment you'll need:

1. Manicure Printing Equipment

    a. Nail Art Printer:
- Description: The core of your business, this device prints designs directly onto nails or nail stickers.
- Types: There are several types of nail art printers including:
  - UV Nail Printers: Use UV light to cure the ink.
  - Inkjet Nail Printers: Use specialized ink cartridges to print designs.
  - Sublimation Printers: Transfer designs using heat.

    b. Printer Accessories:
- Ink Cartridges: Ensure you have a supply of high-quality ink compatible with your printer.

- Nail Art Papers or Stickers: Specially coated papers or stickers designed to be printed and applied to nails.
- Cleaning Kits: For maintaining and cleaning your printer to ensure longevity and consistent quality.

2. Nail Preparation Tools

a. Nail Files and Buffers: To prepare the surface of the nails for printing, ensuring a smooth and even surface.
b. Nail Soakers: For removing old nail polish or products before applying new designs.
c. Cuticle Tools: Tools like cuticle pushers and nippers to prepare nails properly.

3. Application Tools

a. Nail Adhesive: For applying printed stickers or decals to the nail.
b. Top Coat and Base Coat: To protect the printed design and ensure it adheres well.
c. Tweezers: For handling delicate stickers or decals.

4. Finishing Tools

a. UV/LED Lamps: To cure and seal designs when using UV-cured inks or gels.
b. Nail Polish Remover: For cleaning up any excess adhesive or errors.
c. Cleaning Solutions To clean the printer and ensure it operates smoothly.

5. Workspace Setup

a. Workstation: A dedicated area with a clean, organized setup for nail printing and preparation.
  b. Storage: Shelves, drawers, or cabinets to organize printer accessories, nail supplies, and finished products.
  c. Lighting: Proper lighting to ensure accurate color representation and detail work.

6. Business and Marketing Tools
  a. Website or E-commerce Platform: A professional website or online store where customers can place orders, view designs, and learn about your services.
  b. Social Media Accounts: For marketing your services, showcasing designs, and engaging with potential customers.
  c. Photography Equipment: A good camera or smartphone to take high-quality photos of your nail art designs for marketing and promotional purposes.

7. Miscellaneous Tools
  a. Heat Press Machine (if applicable): For sublimation printers, a heat press is used to transfer designs from paper to nails or nail stickers.
  b. Calibration Tools: To ensure that your printer is properly calibrated and producing accurate designs.
  c. Sample Products: Test nails, stickers, or decals to ensure the quality and effectiveness of your printing process.

Additional Tips
1. Training: Ensure you and your staff are well-trained in using the manicure printer and applying designs.
2. Quality Control: Implement strict quality control measures to maintain high standards and customer satisfaction.

By gathering these tools and setting up an organized workspace, you'll be well-equipped to start and run a successful manicure printer business. Focus on delivering high-quality prints and excellent customer service to build a strong reputation and grow your business.

4. Power Bank Vending Machines

With the increasing reliance on mobile devices, power bank vending machines provide on-the-go charging solutions in high-traffic areas. These customizable machines offer cashless payment options, catering to the needs of modern consumers.

Starting a power bank vending machine business involves a mix of vending technology, business operations, and customer service. Here's a comprehensive list of the tools and equipment you'll need to get started:

1. Vending Machines
  a. Power Bank Vending Machines: The primary equipment where customers can rent or purchase power banks.
     Types:
     - Automated Vending Machines: Machines that dispense power banks and accept payments.
     - Smart Vending Machines: Equipped with touch screens, internet connectivity, and tracking systems.
  b. Power Bank Inventory: High-quality, reliable power banks to stock in your vending machines.
     Types:
     - Portable Power Banks: Various capacities to meet different customer needs.

- Charging Cables: To ensure compatibility with different devices (USB-C, Lightning, Micro-USB).

2. Payment and Transaction Systems
a. Payment Processing Systems: Systems for accepting various forms of payment.
Types:
- Cash Acceptors: For machines that accept cash.
- Card Readers: For credit/debit card payments.
- Mobile Payment Systems: For payments through mobile apps like Apple Pay, Google Pay, or QR codes.

b. Receipt Printers: For providing receipts or transaction records to customers.

3. Vending Machine Management Tools
a. Monitoring and Management Software: Software to monitor inventory levels, track sales, and manage machine performance remotely.
Features:
- Real-Time Inventory Tracking: To monitor stock levels and plan restocking.
- Remote Diagnostics: To identify issues or malfunctions.

b. Maintenance Tools: Tools needed for routine maintenance and repair of vending machines.

Examples: Screwdrivers, wrenches, cleaning supplies, and replacement parts.

4. Location and Installation Tools
a. Site Assessment Tools: Tools to evaluate potential vending locations.
   Examples: Measuring tape, cameras for site inspection, and software for analyzing foot traffic.
b. Installation Equipment: Tools for setting up and securing vending machines at selected locations.
   Examples: Bolts, anchors, and tools for leveling and securing machines.

5. Marketing and Promotional Tools
a. Advertising Materials:
   - Description: To promote your vending machine business and attract customers.
   - Flyers and Posters For distribution in the vicinity of your vending machines.
   - Digital Signage: To be displayed on the vending machine screen or at the location.
b. Branding Materials: Items that reflect your business brand.
   Examples: Logos, decals, and custom designs for vending machines.
c. Website and Social Media: Platforms for promoting your business, providing customer support, and sharing updates.

<u>Examples:</u> A professional website, social media accounts, and online marketing campaigns.

6. Customer Service Tools
   a. Customer Support System: To handle customer inquiries, complaints, and support.
   <u>Examples:</u> Phone support, email, and chat systems.
   b. FAQ and Instructional Materials: Information to help customers understand how to use the vending machine and power banks.
   <u>Examples:</u> Instructions on the machine, FAQ sheets, and customer service contact details.

7. Safety and Compliance Tools
   a. Security Systems: To protect your vending machines from theft and vandalism.
   <u>Examples:</u> Security cameras, alarms, and tamper-proof locks.
   b. Compliance Documentation: Ensure that your business meets local regulations and standards.
   <u>Examples:</u> Permits, health and safety certifications, and electrical compliance.

Additional Considerations
- Training: Ensure you and your team are trained in operating and maintaining the vending machines.

- Partnerships: Build relationships with suppliers for power banks and parts, as well as locations for machine placement.
- Customer Feedback: Implement systems to gather and respond to customer feedback for continuous improvement.

By equipping yourself with these tools and setting up a well-organized operation, you'll be well-prepared to launch and run a successful power bank vending machine business.

5. Laser Engraving Machine

Laser engraving machines unlock opportunities in personalized gifts and decorative items. Entrepreneurs can capitalize on their design skills to create unique products for online marketplaces and social media platforms.

Starting a laser engraving machine business involves acquiring the right tools and equipment to ensure high-quality engraving and efficient operations. Here's a comprehensive list of the tools and equipment you'll need:

1. Laser Engraving Equipment
   a. Laser Engraving Machine: The core equipment for your business, used for engraving designs on various materials.
   <u>Types:</u>
   - CO_2 Laser Engravers: Versatile for engraving on wood, acrylic, glass, leather, and some metals.
   - Fiber Laser Engravers: Best for engraving on metals and some plastics.
   - Diode Lasers: Suitable for small-scale or hobbyist applications.

   b. Laser Accessories:
   - Focus Lens: For adjusting the focal point of the laser beam.
   - Engraving Bed: A flat surface where materials are placed during engraving.
   - Rotary Attachment: For engraving cylindrical objects like bottles or pens.

2. Design and Software Tools
   a. Design Software:: Software to create or import designs for engraving.
      <u>Examples:</u>
      - Adobe Illustrator: For vector-based designs.
      - CorelDRAW: Popular for creating and editing engraving designs.
      - Inkscape: A free, open-source vector graphics editor.
   b. Laser Engraving Software: Software that interfaces with your laser machine to control the engraving process.
   <u>Examples</u>: R DWorks, LightBurn, or proprietary software provided by the laser machine manufacturer.

3. Material Handling and Preparation Tools
   a. Material Stock: Different types of materials you will be engraving.
      <u>Examples:</u>
      - Wood: Plywood, MDF, and hardwoods.
      - Acrylic: Clear, colored, and mirrored acrylic sheets.
      - Glass: Drinking glasses, trophies, or awards.
      - Leather: Genuine or synthetic leather for personalization.
   b. Cutting Tools For preparing materials before engraving.
   Examples: Laser cutters (if you plan to cut as well as engrave), utility knives, and rulers.

4. **Maintenance and Safety Equipment**
   a. Cleaning Supplies To maintain the laser engraver and work area.
      Examples: Lens cleaning kits, air compressors for removing dust, and cleaning cloths.
   b. Safety Gear: To protect yourself and your team during operation.
      Examples:
      - Safety Glasses: To protect eyes from laser light.
      - Gloves: To handle materials safely.
      - Fire Extinguisher: For emergency situations.
   c. Ventilation System: To remove fumes and smoke generated by laser engraving.
      Examples: Fume extractors or exhaust fans.

5. **Operational and Business Tools**
   a. Workstation: A dedicated area for your laser engraver and related tasks.
      - Features: Adequate space, sturdy work surface, and proper lighting.
   b. Computer and Accessories: For running design and engraving software.
      Examples: A reliable computer, monitor, mouse, and keyboard.
   c. Inventory Management System: To keep track of materials, finished products, and orders.
      Examples: Inventory management software or spreadsheets.

6. Marketing and Customer Interaction Tools
   a. Website: A professional website to showcase your products, services, and portfolio.
      Features: Online store, contact information, and a gallery of past work.
   b. Social Media: Platforms to market your business and engage with customers.
      Examples: Instagram, Facebook, Pinterest.
   c. Photography Equipment: To take high-quality images of your engraved products for marketing and portfolio purposes.
      Examples: A good camera or smartphone, lighting setup.

7. Miscellaneous Tools
   a. Calibration Tools: For ensuring the laser engraver is correctly calibrated and operating at peak performance.
      Examples: Calibration templates or tools provided by the manufacturer.
   b. Packaging Supplies: For packaging and shipping finished products.
      Examples: Boxes, bubble wrap, and packing materials.
   c. Training Materials: To educate yourself and your staff on operating the laser engraver and handling materials.

      Examples: Manuals, online tutorials, and training courses.

By equipping yourself with these tools and setting up a well-organized workspace, you'll be prepared to start and operate a successful laser engraving machine business. Focus on high-quality craftsmanship and excellent customer service to build a strong reputation and grow your business.

6. Badge Making Machine

Badge making machines facilitate the production of custom-designed badges, catering to diverse markets and occasions. Online platforms serve as effective channels for marketing and sales, enabling entrepreneurs to reach a wide audience.

Starting a badge-making machine business involves a combination of machinery, tools, and supplies to create custom badges. Here's a comprehensive list of the tools and equipment you'll need to set up and run your badge-making business effectively:

1. Badge-Making Equipment

   a. Badge-Making Machines: The core equipment for producing badges. They come in various types based on the size and type of badges you want to create.

   Types
   - Manual Badge-Making Machines: Operated by hand, suitable for small-scale production.
   - Automatic Badge-Making Machines: For higher volume and efficiency, often with electric or pneumatic controls.

- Digital Badge Printers: For printing designs directly onto badge materials.
b. Die Cutters and Punches: Used for cutting badge shapes from materials.
Types:
- Round Die Cutters: Commonly used for circular badges.
- Custom Dies: For unique shapes or custom designs.
c. Heat Press Machines (if applicable): For applying heat-sensitive materials like sublimation transfers onto badges.

2. Printing and Design Tools
a. Design Software: Software for creating and editing badge designs.
Examples:
- Adobe Illustrator: For vector graphics and detailed designs.
- CorelDRAW: Popular for badge design.
- Inkscape: A free, open-source vector graphics editor.

b. Digital Printers: For printing designs onto badge materials.
Types
- Inkjet Printers: Suitable for printing on paper or certain badge materials.
- Laser Printers: For high-quality, durable prints on specialty materials.

c. Printer Accessories: For managing and maintaining printing equipment.

Examples: Ink cartridges, paper or film for printing.

3. Badge Materials and Supplies

a. Badge Blanks: Pre-cut, blank badge bases ready for customization.

Types:
- Metal Blanks: For durable, high-quality badges.
- Plastic Blanks: Cost-effective and lightweight.

b. Badge Components: Parts needed to assemble completed badges.

Examples:
- Pins or Clips: For attaching badges to clothing or accessories.
- Backings: Adhesive or magnetic backings for different badge applications.

c. Lamination Materials: For protecting printed designs and enhancing durability.

Types:
- Lamination Films: Clear films for applying over prints.
- Laminating Machines: For applying the lamination films.

4. Assembly Tools

a. Badge Press: The tool used to assemble the various badge components, such as pressing the printed design onto the badge blank and securing the backing.

b. Hand Tools: Basic tools for manual assembly and adjustments.
Examples: Screwdrivers, tweezers, and pliers.

5. Quality Control and Maintenance Tools

a. Calipers and Rulers: For measuring badge dimensions and ensuring precision.
b. Cleaning Supplies: For maintaining clean equipment and work areas.
Examples: Cleaning cloths, wipes, and solutions.

6. Workspace Setup

a. Workstation: A dedicated, organized area for badge production.
Features: Sturdy work surfaces, adequate lighting, and storage for materials.
b. Storage Solutions: Shelving or cabinets to keep badge materials, components, and finished badges organized.

7. Marketing and Business Tools

a. Website and Online Store: For showcasing your products and enabling online orders.
Features: E-commerce functionality, portfolio of designs, contact information.
b. Social Media Accounts: Platforms for marketing and engaging with customers.
Examples: Facebook, Instagram, LinkedIn.
c. Photography Equipment: For taking high-quality photos of your badges for marketing purposes.

Examples: Camera, lighting setup, photo editing software.

8. **Miscellaneous Tools**
   a. Packaging Supplies: For packaging and shipping finished badges.
      Examples: Boxes, bubble wrap, and packing tape.
   b. Sample Badge Sets: A collection of finished badges to use as samples or prototypes.
   c. Training Materials: For learning about badge-making techniques and machine operation.
      Examples: Manuals, online tutorials, and workshops.

By equipping yourself with these tools and setting up an organized workspace, you'll be well-prepared to start and run a successful badge-making machine business. Focus on quality, customer service, and effective marketing to build a strong brand and grow your business.

7. Engraver Pen

Engraver pens provide a cost-effective solution for personalized gifts and souvenirs. Entrepreneurs can leverage these versatile tools to offer customized products and capitalize on niche markets.

Starting an engraver pen business involves acquiring the right tools and equipment to produce high-quality engraved pens. Here's a detailed list of the tools and supplies you'll need to set up and operate your engraver pen business effectively:

1. Engraving Equipment
   a. Laser Engraving Machine: The primary tool for engraving designs onto pens.
   Types:
   - CO_2 Laser Engraver: Versatile for materials like metal, plastic, and wood.
   - Fiber Laser Engraver: Best for engraving metals with high precision.

   b. Rotary Engraving Machine: Used for engraving cylindrical objects like pens. It can be manual or computer-controlled.
   Features: Includes fixtures and rotary attachments for precise engraving.

   c. Handheld Engraving Tools (if applicable): For manual or custom engraving tasks.
   Types: Rotary tools with engraving bits.

2. Design and Software Tools
   a. Design Software: Software for creating and editing designs to be engraved.

Examples:
- Adobe Illustrator: For vector designs.
- CorelDRAW: Popular for creating engraving designs.
- Inkscape: A free, open-source vector graphics editor.

b. Laser Engraving Software: Software that communicates with your laser or rotary engraver.
Examples: RDWorks, LightBurn, or proprietary software from the engraver manufacturer.

3. Materials and Supplies

a. Engraving Pens: The main product you'll be engraving.
Types:
- Metal Pens: High-quality, durable options.
- Plastic Pens: Cost-effective and versatile.

b. Engraving Blanks: Spare or test pens for practice or prototypes.

c. Cleaning and Maintenance Supplies: For keeping your equipment in good condition.
Examples: Lens cleaning kits, compressed air, and maintenance tools.

4. Assembly and Finishing Tools

a. Pen Assembly Tools: Tools for assembling and disassembling pens.
Examples: Precision screwdrivers and tweezers.

b. Polishing Tools: For giving pens a smooth, professional finish.
Examples: Polishing cloths, buffing compounds.

c. Lubricants and Adhesives: For assembling pens and ensuring smooth operation.
Examples: Pen lubricants, non-permanent adhesives.

5. Quality Control and Measurement Tools

a. Calipers and Rulers: For measuring the dimensions of pens and ensuring engraving accuracy.

b. Magnification Tools: To inspect the quality of engraving and details.
Examples: Magnifying glasses or digital microscopes.

6. Workspace Setup

a. Workstation: A dedicated area for engraving, assembling, and finishing pens.
Features: Sturdy work surface, proper lighting, and ventilation.

b. Storage Solutions: For organizing pens, materials, and tools.
Examples: Shelving, bins, and tool organizers.

7. Marketing and Business Tools

a. Website and E-commerce Platform: A professional website to showcase your products and enable online sales.
Features: Product catalog, shopping cart, and customer contact information.

b. Social Media Accounts: Platforms for marketing and engaging with customers.
      Examples: Facebook, Instagram, LinkedIn.
   c. Photography Equipment: For taking high-quality photos of your engraved pens for marketing purposes.
      Examples: Camera, lighting setup, photo editing software.

8. Miscellaneous Tools
   a. Packaging Supplies: For packaging and shipping finished pens.
      Examples: Boxes, protective wrapping, and packing tape.
   d. Sample Products: Samples or prototypes of engraved pens for demonstrations or testing.
   e. Training Materials: For learning about engraving techniques and equipment operation.
      Examples: Manuals, online tutorials, and workshops.

By gathering these tools and setting up a well-organized workspace, you'll be well-prepared to start and operate a successful engraver pen business. Focus on high-quality craftsmanship, effective marketing, and excellent customer service to build a strong reputation and grow your business.

8. Drones for Video Shooting

Drones equipped with video shooting capabilities cater to diverse industries, including real estate, events, and aerial photography. Entrepreneurs can offer drone services for marketing, surveillance, and entertainment purposes, tapping into a growing market.

Starting a drone business for video shooting involves a mix of high-quality equipment, software, and operational tools. Here's a comprehensive list of the tools and gear you'll need to get started:

1. Drones and Accessories
    a. Drones: High-quality drones equipped with cameras for video shooting.
       Types:
       - Quadcopters: Most common, with multiple rotors for stability.
       - Professional Drones: High-end models with advanced features for high-quality video (e.g., DJI Mavic 3, DJI Inspire 2).
    b. Camera Equipment: High-resolution cameras for capturing video.
       Types:
       - 4K Cameras: For high-definition video quality.
       - Gimbals/Stabilizers: To ensure smooth, shake-free footage.
    c. Spare Parts and Batteries: Essential for maintaining and operating drones.

Examples:
- Extra Batteries: For extended flight times and multiple shoots.
- Propellers: Spare propellers for quick replacements.
- Chargers: For recharging batteries.

   d. Remote Controllers: For controlling the drone and camera during flight.
Features: Typically includes controls for camera settings, flight paths, and emergency functions.

   e. Storage and Transport Cases: To protect and transport your drones and accessories.
Types:
- Hard Cases: For safe transport.
- Backpacks: For easy carrying and access.

2. Software and Apps
   a. Drone Control Software Software used for planning and controlling drone flights.
   Examples:
   - DJI Go 4: For DJI drones.
   - Litchi: For advanced flight planning and control.

   b. Video Editing Software: For editing and enhancing video footage.
   Examples:
   - Adobe Premiere Pro: Professional-grade video editing.
   - Final Cut Pro: Advanced editing for Mac users.

- DaVinci Resolve: Comprehensive editing with color correction features.
  c. Flight Planning Apps: For planning flight routes and ensuring safe operations.
     Examples:
     - AirMap: For airspace information and flight planning.
     - DroneDeploy: For mapping and automated flight planning.
3. Regulatory and Safety Tools
   a. FAA Registration and Licensing: Ensure your drones are registered and you have the necessary certifications.
      Requirements: Part 107 Certification: For commercial drone operations in the U.S.
   b. Insurance: To cover liability and potential damage or loss.
      Types:
      - Drone Insurance: Specific coverage for drones and related equipment.
      - General Liability Insurance For overall business protection.
   c. Safety Gear: For personal safety and compliance.
      Examples:
      - High-Visibility Clothing: For visibility in outdoor environments.
      - First Aid Kit: For emergency situations.
4. Operational and Business Tools
   a. Workstation: A dedicated area for video editing and administrative tasks.

Features: Desk, computer, and comfortable seating.
   b. **Computer and Accessories**: For video editing and software applications.
   Examples: High-performance computer, monitor, mouse, and keyboard.
   c. **Storage Solutions**: For storing video footage and project files.
   Examples:
   - External Hard Drives: For large video files.
   - Cloud Storage: For backup and easy access.
5. Marketing and Customer Interaction Tools
   a. **Website**: A professional website to showcase your services and portfolio.
   Features: Service descriptions, gallery of work, contact information, and booking options.
   b. **Social Media Accounts**: Platforms for marketing and engaging with clients.
   Examples: Instagram, Facebook, YouTube, LinkedIn.
   c. **Photography Equipment**: For capturing high-quality images of your drone setup and video shoots.
   Examples: Camera, tripod, lighting equipment.
6. Miscellaneous Tools
   a. Drone Maintenance Tools: For keeping drones in good working order.

    <u>Examples</u>: Screwdrivers, replacement parts, and cleaning supplies.
  b. Training Materials: For learning about drone operations and video shooting techniques.
    <u>Examples:</u> Manuals, online tutorials, and industry courses.

By acquiring these tools and setting up an organized workspace, you'll be well-prepared to start and run a successful drone business for video shooting. Focus on high-quality production, safety, and effective marketing to build a strong client base and grow your business.

9. Hydroponic Farming Kits

Hydroponic farming kits enable individuals to grow fresh produce indoors, regardless of climate or space constraints. Entrepreneurs can capitalize on the growing interest in sustainable agriculture by offering comprehensive kits and educational resources.

Starting a hydroponic farming business involves investing in specialized equipment and tools to create an efficient and productive growing environment. Hydroponic systems use nutrient-rich water instead of soil, and the setup requires careful planning and the right tools. Here's a comprehensive list of tools and equipment you'll need:

1. Hydroponic Systems
   a. Hydroponic Growing Systems: The core of your hydroponic setup, providing the environment for plants to grow.
      Types:
      - Deep Water Culture (DWC): Plants are suspended in nutrient-rich water with air stones providing oxygen.
      - Nutrient Film Technique (NFT): A thin film of nutrient solution flows over plant roots.
      - Ebb and Flow (Flood and Drain) Plants are periodically flooded with nutrient solution and then drained.

- Drip System: Nutrient solution is delivered directly to plant roots through drippers.
- Wick System: Nutrient solution is transported to plant roots through wicks.

b. Growing Containers: Pots or trays where plants are supported and grown.
Examples: Net pots, grow bags, or trays.

c. Grow Lights: Provides the necessary light spectrum for plant growth.
Types:
- LED Grow Lights: Energy-efficient and customizable light spectrum.
- Fluorescent Lights: Suitable for seedlings and vegetative growth.
- High-Intensity Discharge (HID) Lights:*Includes Metal Halide (MH) and High-Pressure Sodium (HPS) lamps.

2. Nutrient Delivery and Management

a. Nutrient Solution:A mixture of water and nutrients essential for plant growth.
Types: Pre-mixed nutrient solutions or individual nutrient components (e.g., nitrogen, phosphorus, potassium).

b. pH and EC Meters: To measure the pH level and electrical conductivity (EC) of the nutrient solution.
Examples: Digital pH meters, EC meters.

c. pH Adjusters: Chemicals used to adjust the pH of the nutrient solution.
Examples: pH up and pH down solutions.

3. Environmental Control

    a. Temperature and Humidity Control: Equipment to maintain optimal growing conditions.

    <u>Examples:</u>
- Heaters and Coolers: For temperature regulation.
- Dehumidifiers: To control humidity levels.
- Humidifiers: To increase humidity as needed.

    b. Ventilation and Air Circulation: Ensures proper airflow and prevents mold or fungal issues.

    <u>Examples:</u>
- Fans: Oscillating fans or inline fans.
- Air Filters: To remove dust and contaminants from the air.

    c. Carbon Dioxide (CO_2) Enrichment: Increases CO_2 levels to enhance plant growth (optional, depending on scale).
    <u>Examples:</u> CO_2 generators or tanks.

4. Water Management

    a. Water Pumps: Pumps to circulate and deliver nutrient solutions.

    <u>Types:</u>
- Submersible Pumps: For deep water culture or reservoir systems.
- Inline Pumps: For drip systems or flood and drain systems.

b. Reservoirs and Tanks: Containers for holding nutrient solutions.
      Types: Plastic or metal tanks with sufficient capacity for your system.
   c. Water Filtration Systems: To ensure water quality by removing contaminants.
      Types: Activated carbon filters, reverse osmosis systems.

5. **Support Structures and Accessories**
   a. Plant Supports: Supports to help plants grow upright and healthy.
      Examples: Trellises, stakes, or plant ties.
   b. Growing Medium: Medium to support plant roots in the absence of soil.
      Examples: Rock wool, coconut coir, perlite, vermiculite.
   c. Timers and Controllers: To automate lighting, watering, and nutrient delivery schedules.
      Examples: Digital timers, programmable controllers.

6. **Maintenance and Monitoring Tools**
   a. Cleaning Supplies: For maintaining system hygiene and preventing disease.
      Examples: Brushes, disinfectants, and cleaning solutions.
   b. Monitoring Equipment To keep track of system performance and environmental conditions.
      Examples: Thermometers, hygrometers, data loggers.

7. Workspace Setup
  a. Growing Area: A dedicated space for your hydroponic system, can be in your house or a green house.
  <u>Features</u>: Adequate lighting, ventilation, and access for maintenance.
  b. Storage Solutions: For organizing tools, nutrients, and other supplies.
  <u>Examples:</u> Shelving units, bins, and containers.

8. Marketing and Sales Tools
  a. Website and E-commerce Platform: For showcasing your products and services, and facilitating online sales. Very important for sales.
  <u>Features:</u> Product catalog, online ordering, contact information.
  b. Social Media Accounts: Platforms for marketing and engaging with potential customers.
  <u>Examples</u>: Instagram, Facebook, LinkedIn.
  c. Photography Equipment: For capturing high-quality images of your hydroponic setup and products.
  <u>Examples:</u> Camera, lighting setup, photo editing software.

By acquiring these tools and setting up a well-organized hydroponic farming system, you'll be well-prepared to start and run a successful hydroponic farming business. Focus on quality, efficiency, and effective marketing to build a strong reputation and grow your business.

10. Subscription Box Service

Subscription box services cater to niche markets by offering curated products and experiences on a recurring basis. Entrepreneurs can leverage e-commerce platforms to reach customers globally and build a loyal subscriber base.

Starting a subscription box service involves a range of tools and equipment for product sourcing, packaging, distribution, and customer management. Here's a comprehensive list of tools and supplies you'll need to get started:

1. Business Setup
   a. Business Plan: A detailed plan outlining your business model, target market, financial projections, and operational strategies.
   b. Business Registration and Licenses: Legal requirements for operating your subscription box service.
   Examples: Business license, tax ID number, and any industry-specific permits.

2. Product Sourcing and Management
   a. Product Inventory: The items you will include in your subscription boxes. Monthly boxes can be anything you want: clothes, sox, shavers, creativity at your fingertips.
   Types: Products from suppliers, manufacturers, or custom items.
   b. Supplier Relationships: Building and managing relationships with vendors or manufacturers for sourcing products.

c. Inventory Management Software: Software to track and manage inventory levels and orders.
   Examples: TradeGecko, NetSuite, or inFlow.
3. **Packaging and Fulfillment**
   a. Packaging Supplies: Materials for packing your subscription boxes.
   Examples:
   - Boxes: Various sizes of sturdy cardboard boxes.
   - Filler Materials: Packing peanuts, bubble wrap, tissue paper.
   - Shipping Labels: For labeling and tracking packages.
   - Seals and Tape: To secure packages.
   - Custom Packaging: Branded boxes, inserts, or wrapping.
   b. Packing Stations: A dedicated area for assembling and packing boxes. Some use a storage unit.
   Features: Workbench, packaging supplies, and labeling equipment.
   c. Fulfillment Centers (optional): Outsourced services for warehousing, packing, and shipping your subscription boxes. This is the easiest but if you include in your markup pricing a good way to scale the business.
4. **E-commerce Platform and Tools**
   a. Website and E-commerce Platform: A professional website to manage subscriptions and facilitate online orders.

Features: Subscription management, payment processing, and customer account access.
Examples: Shopify, WooCommerce, BigCommerce.Etsy
  b. Subscription Management Software: Tools to handle recurring billing, customer subscriptions, and analytics.
Examples: ReCharge, Bold Subscriptions, Subbly.
  c. Payment Gateway To process online payments securely.
Examples: PayPal, Stripe, Square.

5. Marketing and Customer Acquisition

  a. Marketing Tools: Tools to promote your subscription box service and attract customers.

Examples:
- Social Media Management: Tools like Hootsuite or Buffer for scheduling and managing social media posts.
- Email Marketing: Tools like Mailchimp or Klaviyo for sending promotional emails and newsletters.
- Content Creation: Graphic design tools like Canva or Adobe Creative Suite.

  b. Customer Relationship Management (CRM): To manage customer interactions and track sales.
Examples: HubSpot, Zoho CRM.

c. Influencer and Affiliate Programs: Programs to collaborate with influencers and affiliates to promote your subscription boxes.

6. **Shipping and Logistics**
   a. Shipping Software:Tools to streamline the shipping process, print labels, and track packages.
   Examples: ShipStation, Shippo, Easyship.
   b. Shipping Carriers:Services for delivering your boxes to customers.
   Examples: UPS, FedEx, USPS, DHL.
   c. Tracking and Delivery Management: Tools to provide customers with tracking information and manage delivery issues.

7. **Customer Service Tools**
   a. Customer Support Software: Tools to handle customer inquiries, complaints, and feedback.
   Examples: Zendesk, Freshdesk, Help Scout.

   b. Live Chat Tools: For real-time customer support on your website.
   Examples: Intercom, Drift.

8. **Miscellaneous Tools**
   a. Market Research Tools: For understanding your target market and refining your product offerings.
   Examples: Surveys, focus groups, Google Analytics.
   b. Data Analytics Tools:For analyzing customer behavior and business performance.

>   <u>Examples:</u> Google Analytics, Tableau.
> c. Packaging Desig To create custom designs for your subscription boxes.
>   <u>Examples:</u> Graphic design software or hiring a designer.

By gathering these tools and setting up efficient processes, you'll be well-prepared to start and manage a successful subscription box service. Focus on product quality, customer satisfaction, and effective marketing to build a strong customer base and grow your business.

11. DIY Candle Making Kits

DIY candle making kits provide a creative outlet for hobbyists and enthusiasts interested in home decor and aromatherapy. By offering comprehensive kits with high-quality materials, entrepreneurs can tap into the growing demand for handmade products. Starting a DIY candle-making business requires a variety of tools and supplies to ensure you can produce high-quality candles efficiently and safely. Here's a comprehensive list of tools and equipment you'll need:

1. Candle Making Tools and Equipment

    a. Melting Pots: Used for melting wax.
    <u>Types:</u>
- Double Boiler: For melting wax gently without direct heat.
- Wax Melter: For larger batches, with temperature control.

    b. Wax: The primary material used to make candles.
    <u>Types:</u>
- Paraffin Wax: Common and affordable, but less eco-friendly.
- Soy Wax: Made from soybeans, a popular eco-friendly option.
- Beeswax: Natural and has a pleasant honey scent.
- Palm Wax: Sustainable and produces a unique texture.

c. **Fragrance Oils:** For adding scents to your candles.
   <u>Types</u>: Choose high-quality, candle-safe fragrance oils.
d. **Dye:** For coloring candles. (optional)
   Types:**
   - Liquid Dyes: Easy to mix into melted wax.
   - Dye Chips: Solid form, melted into the wax.

e. **Wicks:** The part of the candle that burns.
   <u>Types</u>:
   - Cotton Wicks: Commonly used, good for most waxes.
   - Wood Wicks: Provide a crackling effect and unique appearance.
   - Metal Core Wicks: Stabilize the wick, but less common in eco-friendly candles.
f. **Wick Holders:** Devices to keep the wick centered while the wax sets.
   <u>Types:</u> Wick stickers, metal or wooden wick holders.
g. **Pouring Pitcher:** For pouring melted wax into molds or containers.
h. **Thermometer:** To monitor the temperature of melted wax.
i. **Scale:** For measuring wax, fragrance, and dye accurately.
j. **Stirring Utensils:** For mixing fragrance oils and dye into the wax.

Types: Wooden or silicone spatulas.

2. Molds and Containers
a. Candle Molds: Used to shape candles.
   Types:
   - Silicone Molds: Flexible and easy to release candles.
   - Metal Molds: Durable and reusable.
   - Plastic Molds: Lightweight and cost-effective.

b. Candle Containers: For container candles. Types: Glass jars, tins, ceramic holders, or any heat-resistant container.

3. Safety Equipment
a. Heat-Resistant Gloves: For handling hot wax and equipment safely.
b. Safety Glasses: To protect your eyes from any potential splashes.
c. Fire Extinguisher: For safety in case of a fire.

4. Workspace Setup
a. Work Surface: A clean, heat-resistant area for candle making.
b. Drop Cloths or Newspaper: To protect your work area from spills and stains.
c. Cleaning Supplies: For cleaning up after candle making.
   Examples: Paper towels, sponges, and mild cleaners.

5. Packaging and Labeling
a. Packaging Materials: To package your candles for sale.

Examples: Boxes, bags, tissue paper, and bubble wrap.
  b. Labels and Branding: To brand your candles and provide product information.
     Types:
     - Custom Labels: With your logo, candle scent, and other details.
     - Labeling Machine: For efficiency in labeling large quantities.

  c. Tagging Supplies: Tags with product information or branding.
     Examples: String tags, adhesive tags.

6. Marketing and Sales Tools
   a. Website and E-commerce Platform: For showcasing and selling your candles online.
      Examples: Shopify, WooCommerce, BigCommerce, Etsy
   b. Social Media Accounts: To promote your products and engage with customers.
      Examples: Instagram, Facebook, Pinterest.
   c. Photography Equipment: For high-quality images of your candles for marketing.
      Examples: Camera, lighting setup, photo editing software.

7. **Miscellaneous Tools**
   a. Market Research Tools: To understand your market and refine your product offerings.
      Examples: Surveys, focus groups, Google Analytics.

b. **Data Analytics Tools:** For analyzing sales performance and customer behavior. <u>Examples:</u> Google Analytics, Tableau.

By gathering these tools and supplies, you'll be well-equipped to start and run a successful DIY candle-making business. Focus on product quality, safety, and effective marketing to build a strong customer base and grow your business.

12. Personalized Phone Cases

Personalized phone cases offer a lucrative opportunity for entrepreneurs with design skills and creativity. By leveraging print-on-demand services and e-commerce platforms, entrepreneurs can reach a global audience and capitalize on customization trends.

Starting a personalized phone case business requires a variety of tools and equipment to design, customize, and produce phone cases. Here's a comprehensive list of the essential tools and supplies you'll need:

1. Design and Customization Tools
   a. Graphic Design Software: For creating and editing designs for phone cases.
   Examples: Adobe Illustrator, Adobe Photoshop, CorelDRAW, Canva.
   b. Design Templates: Pre-designed templates to streamline the customization process.
   Examples: Templates for different phone case models and sizes.
   c. Digital Drawing Tablet: For creating detailed and precise designs.
   Examples: Wacom, Huion.

2. Printing and Production Equipment
   a. Printer: For printing designs onto phone case materials.
   Types:
   - Sublimation Printer: For transferring designs onto coated cases using heat.

- UV Printer: For direct printing onto hard phone cases using UV light.

b. Heat Press Machine: To apply heat and pressure to transfer designs onto phone cases.

Types:
- Flat Heat Press: For pressing designs onto flat surfaces like phone cases.
- 3D Heat Press: For cases with curved surfaces.

c. Cutting Machine: For cutting designs from vinyl or other materials.

Examples: Cricut Maker, Silhouette Cameo.

3. Phone Case Materials

a. Blank Phone Cases: Base phone cases that you will personalize.

Types:
- Plastic Cases: Commonly used for sublimation or UV printing.
- Silicone Cases: Flexible and often used for custom designs.
- Leather or Faux Leather Cases: For a premium look and feel.

b. Sublimation Paper: Special paper for transferring sublimation ink designs onto phone cases.

c. Transfer Sheets or Films: Used with UV printing or vinyl cutting to transfer designs.

4. Finishing and Quality Control Tools

a. Protective Coatings: To protect printed designs and enhance durability.

Examples: Clear acrylic spray or laminate sheets.
   b. Quality Control Tools: For checking the quality and consistency of finished phone cases.
   Examples: Magnifying glass, color calibration tools.

5. Packaging and Shipping
   a. Packaging Materials: For packaging your phone cases attractively and securely.
   Examples: Custom boxes, protective sleeves, bubble wrap.
   b. Shipping Supplies: For sending phone cases to customers.
   Examples: Shipping labels, poly mailers, packing tape.
   c. Shipping Software: For managing shipping and tracking orders.
   Examples: ShipStation, Shippo.

6. Sales and Customer Management
   a. E-commerce Platform: For setting up an online store to sell your phone cases.
   Examples: Shopify, WooCommerce, BigCommerce, Etsy
   b. Payment Gateway: To process payments online.
   Examples: PayPal, Stripe, Square.
   c. Customer Relationship Management (CRM) Software: For managing customer interactions and tracking sales.
   Examples: HubSpot, Zoho CRM.

7. Marketing Tools
   a. Social Media Accounts: Platforms to promote your products and engage with customers.
      <u>Examples</u>: Instagram, Facebook, Pinterest.

   b. Email Marketing Tools: For sending promotional emails and newsletters.
      <u>Examples</u>: Mailchimp, Klaviyo.
   c. Photography Equipment: For taking high-quality images of your phone cases for marketing.
      <u>Examples:</u> Camera, lighting setup, photo editing software.

8. Workspace Setup
   a. Workbench or Table: A dedicated area for designing, printing, and assembling phone cases.
   b. Storage Solutions: For organizing phone cases, materials, and tools.
      <u>Examples:</u> Shelving units, bins, and drawers.
   c. Cleaning Supplies: For maintaining a clean and organized workspace.
      <u>Examples:</u> Cloths, cleaning solutions, and organizers.

By gathering these tools and setting up a well-organized workspace, you'll be prepared to start and run a successful personalized phone case business. Focus on high-quality designs, efficient production processes, and effective marketing to build a strong customer base and grow your business.

13. Handmade Soap Production

Handmade soap production appeals to consumers seeking natural and eco-friendly skincare products. Entrepreneurs can experiment with ingredients and scents to create unique formulations, catering to diverse preferences.

Starting a handmade soap production business requires a variety of tools and supplies for creating, curing, and packaging your products. Here's a comprehensive list of the essential tools and equipment you'll need:

1. Soap Making Tools and Equipment
   a. Soap Molds: Molds to shape your soap into bars or other forms.
   Types:
   - Silicone Molds: Flexible and easy to release soaps.
   - Wooden Molds: Durable and typically used for larger batches.
   - Plastic Molds: Various shapes and sizes for different soap designs.

   b. Mixing Containers: Containers for mixing soap ingredients.
   Types:
   - -Heat-Resistant Bowls: For handling hot lye and oils.
   - Stainless Steel or Plastic: Avoid reactive materials like aluminum.

   c. Measuring Tools: For accurately measuring ingredients.
   Examples:

- Digital Scales: For precise measurement of oils, lye, and additives.
- Measuring Cups and Spoons: For smaller quantities and additives.

d. Stick Blender: For blending soap ingredients until they reach "trace" (the point where the mixture thickens and holds a shape).
e. Thermometer: To monitor the temperature of oils and lye solution.
<u>Types:</u>
Digital Thermometer: For quick and accurate readings.
f. Safety Equipment: To ensure safe handling of ingredients and equipment.
Examples:
   - Protective Gloves: To protect your hands from lye and other chemicals.
   - Safety Glasses: To protect your eyes from splashes.
   - Aprons: To keep your clothing protected.
g. Lye (Sodium Hydroxide): Essential for the saponification process (turning oils into soap). Handle with care and follow safety guidelines.
h. Oils and Butters: Base ingredients for soap.
<u>Examples:</u> Olive oil, coconut oil, palm oil, shea butter, cocoa butter.
i. Additives: Ingredients to enhance your soap's properties or appearance.
<u>Types:</u>

- Fragrance Oils: For adding scent to your soap.
- Essential Oils: Natural oils for fragrance and therapeutic benefits.
- Colorants: Natural or synthetic colorants for visual appeal.

<u>Exfoliants:</u> Such as oatmeal, coffee grounds, or seeds.

j. Soap Cutter: To cut large blocks of soap into bars.

<u>Types:</u>
- Wire Cutter: For precise cuts.
- Bench Cutter: For larger batches.

2. Curing and Storage

a. Curing Racks or Shelves: To allow soap to cure and harden.

<u>Types:</u>

Wire Racks: Allow for good airflow around the soap.

b. Storage Containers: For storing ingredients and finished soap.

<u>Types:</u>

Airtight Containers: To keep ingredients fresh and prevent contamination.

3. Packaging and Labeling

a. Packaging Materials: For wrapping and presenting your soaps.

<u>Examples::</u>
- Paper Wrapping: Kraft paper, wax paper.
- Boxes: Custom or pre-made boxes for soap bars.

- Bags: Cellophane or fabric bags.
  b. Labels and Branding: To identify and market your soap products.

  Examples:
  - Custom Labels: With product name, ingredients, and branding.
  - Labeling Machine: For efficiency in labeling large quantities.
  c. Heat Sealer (optional): For sealing bags or wrappers.

4. Marketing and Sales
  a. E-commerce Platform: For selling your soap online.
     Examples: Shopify, WooCommerce, Etsy.
  b. Social Media Accounts: To promote your products and engage with customers.
     Examples: Instagram, Facebook, Pinterest.
  c. Photography Equipment: For taking high-quality images of your soap products.
     Examples: Camera, lighting setup, photo editing software.

5. Workspace Setup
  a. Work Surface: A clean, organized area for soap making.
     Features: Heat-resistant and easy to clean.
  b. Storage Solutions: For organizing tools, ingredients, and finished products.
     Examples: Shelving units, bins, and drawers.
  c. Cleaning Supplies: For maintaining a clean workspace.

Examples: Cloths, cleaning solutions, and scrub brushes.

7. Miscellaneous Tools

a. Market Research Tools: To understand your market and refine your product offerings.
Examples: Surveys, focus groups, Google Analytics.

b. Data Analytics Tools: For analyzing sales performance and customer behavior.
Examples: Google Analytics, Tableau.

By gathering these tools and setting up an organized workspace, you'll be well-prepared to start and run a successful handmade soap production business. Focus on product quality, safety, and effective marketing to build a strong customer base and grow your business.

14. Vertical Garden Kits

Vertical garden kits enable individuals to create green spaces in urban environments, promoting sustainability and wellness. Entrepreneurs can offer comprehensive kits and installation services to homeowners, businesses, and community organizations.

Starting a vertical gardening kit business involves several tools and supplies to design, assemble, and package your kits effectively. Here's a comprehensive list of what you'll need:

1. Design and Planning Tools
   a. Design Software: For creating plans and prototypes of your vertical garden kits.
   <u>Examples:</u> SketchUp, Adobe Illustrator, Canva.
   b. Prototyping Tools: For building and testing initial designs.
   <u>Examples:</u> Basic carpentry tools, 3D printers for prototype parts.

2. Manufacturing and Assembly Tools
   a. Vertical Garden Components: Essential parts of the kits.
   <u>Examples:</u>
- Planters/Pots: Containers for plants, typically modular or stackable.
- Mounting Systems: Frames, brackets, or wall mounts to secure planters.
- Irrigation System: Drip hoses or water reservoirs if included in the kit.

- Growing Medium: Soil or hydroponic medium like coconut coir or peat moss.
- Seeds or Seedlings: Depending on the kit's focus.

  b. Cutting and Drilling Tools: For shaping and preparing components.
<u>Examples:</u> Saw, drill, jigsaw.

  c. Assembly Tools: For putting together the kits.
<u>Examples:</u> Screwdrivers, pliers, wrenches.

  d. Adhesives and Fasteners: For securing parts.
<u>Examples:</u> Screws, nails, glue, or brackets.

3. Quality Control and Testing

  a. Measurement Tools: For ensuring accuracy and quality.
<u>Examples:</u> Rulers, tape measures, levels.

  b. Testing Equipment: For testing the functionality of the vertical garden systems.
<u>Examples:</u> Water flow testers, weight scales.

4. Packaging and Shipping

  a. Packaging Materials: For protecting and presenting your kits.
<u>Examples:</u> Boxes, bubble wrap, packing peanuts, instruction manuals.

  b. Labeling Tools: For identifying and branding your kits.
<u>Examples:</u> Custom labels, stickers.

  c. Shipping Supplies: For sending kits to customers.
<u>Examples:</u> Shipping boxes, tape, shipping labels.

d. Shipping Software: For managing shipping and tracking.
      Examples: ShipStation, Shippo.
5. **Marketing and Sales Tools**
   a. E-commerce Platform: For selling your kits online.
      Examples: Shopify, WooCommerce, Etsy.
   b. Social Media Accounts:To promote your kits and engage with customers.
      Examples: Instagram, Facebook, Pinterest.
   c. Photography Equipment: For taking high-quality images of your kits.
      Examples: Camera, lighting setup.
   d. Website and Marketing Materials: For creating an online presence and marketing your kits.
      Examples: Website, brochures, flyers.
6. **Workspace Setup**
   a. Workbench or Assembly Area: A clean and organized space for assembling kits.
      Features: Adequate lighting, tools storage, and work surfaces.
   b. Storage Solutions: For organizing components and finished kits.
      Examples: Shelving units, bins, and drawers.
   c. Cleaning Supplies: For maintaining a tidy workspace.
      Examples: Cloths, cleaning solutions.
7. **Miscellaneous Tools**
   a. Market Research Tools: To understand your market and refine your product offerings.

<u>Examples:</u> Surveys, focus groups.
b. Data Analytics Tools: For analyzing sales and customer behavior.
<u>Examples:</u> Google Analytics, Tableau.

By gathering these tools and setting up a well-organized workspace, you'll be prepared to start and run a successful vertical gardening kit business. Focus on high-quality components, efficient assembly, and effective marketing to attract and retain customers.

15. Aquaponics Systems

Aquaponics systems combine aquaculture and hydroponics to create sustainable ecosystems for growing fish and plants. Entrepreneurs can offer turnkey solutions for home and commercial use, tapping into the growing demand for organic produce.

Starting an aquaponics system business requires a variety of tools and equipment for designing, building, and maintaining the systems, as well as for growing and harvesting plants and fish. Here's a comprehensive list of what you'll need:

1. **Design and Planning Tools**
    a. Design Software: For creating and planning aquaponics system layouts.
       Examples: AutoCAD, SketchUp, Microsoft Visio.
    b. Prototyping Tools: For testing system designs and setups.
       Examples: Basic carpentry tools, 3D printer for prototypes.

2. **System Components**
    a. Grow Beds: Containers for growing plants.
       Types:
       - Media Beds: Filled with grow media like expanded clay pellets.
       - Raft Systems: Floating beds for plants in a nutrient-rich solution.
       - NFT Channels: Nutrient Film Technique channels for plant roots.

b. Fish Tanks: Tanks for housing fish.
   <u>Types:</u>
   - Circular Tanks: For efficient water circulation.
   - Rectangular Tanks: Common for easier placement and maintenance.
c. Water Pumps: For circulating water between fish tanks and grow beds.
   <u>Types:</u> Submersible or external pumps depending on system size.
d. Air Pumps and Aerators: To provide oxygen to fish and plants.
   <u>Types</u>: Air stones, diffusers.
e. Filtration Systems: To filter solids and maintain water quality.
   <u>Types:</u> Mechanical filters, biofilters, and UV sterilizers.
f. Plumbing Components: For water distribution and drainage.
   <u>Types:</u> PVC pipes, fittings, valves, hoses.

3. Water Quality Management
a. Water Testing Kits: For monitoring water parameters like pH, ammonia, nitrites, and nitrates.
   <u>Examples:</u> Test strips, digital testers.
b. Water Treatment Supplies: For adjusting water quality and nutrient levels.
   <u>Examples</u>: pH adjusters, de-chlorinators.
c. Heating and Cooling Equipment: To maintain optimal water temperatures.
   <u>Types:</u> Heaters, chillers.

4. **Growing Medium and Nutrients**
   a. Growing Media: Medium in which plants grow.
      Examples: Expanded clay pellets, gravel, perlite.
   b. Fertilizers and Supplements: To provide additional nutrients as needed.
      Types: Organic or hydroponic fertilizers.
5. **Harvesting Tools**
   a. Harvesting Equipment: For collecting plants and fish.
      Types: Scissors, nets, containers.
   b. Scales: For weighing harvested fish and produce.
6. **Packaging and Storage**
   a. Packaging Materials: For packaging produce and fish.
      Types: Boxes, bags, or containers.
   b. Storage Solutions: For storing components, harvested produce, and fish.
      Examples: Shelving units, coolers.
7. **Marketing and Sales Tools**
   a. E-commerce Platform: For selling systems, components, or produce online.
      Examples: Shopify, WooCommerce, Etsy.
   b. Social Media Accounts: To promote your business and engage with customers.
      Examples: Instagram, Facebook, Pinterest.
   c. Photography Equipment: For capturing high-quality images of your systems and produce.
      Examples: Camera, lighting setup.

d. Website and Marketing Materials: For creating an online presence and marketing your products.
      Examples: Website, brochures, flyers.

8. Workspace Setup
   a. Workbench or Assembly Area: A clean, organized space for setting up and maintaining systems.
      Features: Adequate lighting, tools storage.
   b. Storage Solutions: For organizing tools, components, and supplies.
      Examples: Shelving units, bins.
   c. Cleaning Supplies: For maintaining a clean workspace.

10. Miscellaneous Tools
   a. Market Research Tools: To understand your market and refine your product offerings.
      Examples: Surveys, focus groups.
   b. Data Analytics Tools: For analyzing sales performance and customer behavior.
      Examples: Google Analytics, Tableau.

By gathering these tools and setting up a well-organized workspace, you'll be ready to start and run a successful aquaponics system business. Focus on system efficiency, quality control, and effective marketing to attract and retain customers.

16. Digital Marketing Consultancy

Digital marketing consultancy services cater to businesses seeking expertise in online branding, advertising, and lead generation. Entrepreneurs with experience in SEO, social media, and content marketing can offer specialized services to clients across industries.

Starting a digital marketing agency involves several key tools and resources to effectively plan, execute, and manage digital marketing campaigns for clients. Here's a comprehensive list of the tools and equipment you'll need to get started:

1. Strategy and Planning Tools
   a. Market Research Tools: For understanding market trends, competition, and audience needs.
      Examples: Google Trends, SEMrush, Ahrefs, BuzzSumo.
   b. Project Management Tools: For managing projects, tasks, and team collaboration.
      Examples: Asana, Trello, Monday.com, ClickUp.
   c. Business Strategy Software: For creating and tracking business plans and strategies.
      Examples: LivePlan, Strategyzer.

2. Website and SEO Tools
   a. Website Builders and CMS: For creating and managing websites.
      Examples: WordPress, Squarespace, Wix.
   b. SEO Tools: For optimizing websites and tracking SEO performance.

<u>Examples</u>: Google Search Console, Moz, Screaming Frog SEO Spider.
   c. Keyword Research Tools: For identifying relevant keywords and optimizing content.
   <u>Examples</u>: Google Keyword Planner, Ubersuggest.
   d. Analytics Tools: For tracking and analyzing website and campaign performance.
   <u>Examples</u>: Google Analytics, Matomo.

3. Content Creation Tools
   a. Graphic Design Software: For creating visual content like social media graphics, infographics, and ads.
   <u>Examples</u>: Adobe Creative Suite (Photoshop, Illustrator), Canva.
   b. Video Editing Software: For producing and editing video content.
   <u>Examples</u>: Adobe Premiere Pro, Final Cut Pro, DaVinci Resolve. There are free programs to start your business and move to these paid ones.
   c. Copywriting Tools: For creating compelling marketing copy and content.
   <u>Examples</u>: Grammarly, Hemingway Editor.

4. Social Media Management Tools
   a. Social Media Scheduling Tools: For scheduling and managing posts across multiple platforms.
   <u>Examples</u>: Hootsuite, Buffer, Later.
   b. Social Media Analytics Tools: For tracking social media performance and engagement.

Examples: Sprout Social, Socialbakers.
   c. Social Media Ad Management: For creating and managing social media advertising campaigns.
   Examples: Facebook Ads Manager, LinkedIn Campaign Manager.

5. **Email Marketing Tools**
   a. Email Marketing Platforms: For creating, sending, and tracking email campaigns.
   Examples: Mailchimp, Sendinblue, Constant Contact.
   b. Automation Tools: For automating email sequences and marketing workflows.
   Examples: HubSpot, ActiveCampaign.

6. **Advertising and PPC Tools**
   a. Pay-Per-Click (PPC) Advertising Platforms: For managing and optimizing paid search and display ads.
   Examples: Google Ads, Bing Ads.
   b. Ad Tracking and Analytics Tools: For tracking the performance of ad campaigns.
   Examples: Google Analytics, AdEspresso.

7. **Client Management and CRM Tools**
   a. CRM Software: For managing client relationships and sales pipelines.
   Examples: HubSpot CRM, Salesforce, Zoho CRM.
   b. Proposal and Contract Management: For creating and managing client proposals and contracts.
   Examples: PandaDoc, Proposify.

8. Communication and Collaboration Tools
   a. Communication Platforms: For internal and client communication.
      Examples: Slack, Microsoft Teams, Zoom.
   b. File Sharing and Storage: For sharing and storing files securely.
      Examples: Google Drive, Dropbox, OneDrive.

9. Administrative Tools
   a. Time Tracking Tools: For tracking time spent on projects and billing clients.
      Examples: Toggl, Harvest.

10. Marketing and Sales Tools
   a. Marketing Automation Platforms: For automating marketing tasks and campaigns.
      Examples: HubSpot, Marketo.
   b. Sales Funnels and Landing Pages: For creating high-converting landing pages and sales funnels.
      Examples: ClickFunnels, Unbounce.
   c. Analytics and Reporting Tools: For generating reports and insights on marketing performance.
      Examples: Google Data Studio, Tableau.

11. Workspace Setup
   a. Office Equipment: Essential for daily operations.
      Examples: Computers, printers, office furniture.

b. Ergonomic Workspace: To ensure a comfortable and productive working environment.
Examples: Ergonomic chairs, adjustable desks.

By gathering these tools and setting up an organized workspace, you'll be well-equipped to start and run a successful digital marketing agency. Focus on delivering high-quality services, building strong client relationships, and leveraging effective marketing strategies to grow your business.

17. Remote Tech Support

Remote tech support services provide timely assistance to individuals and businesses facing technical issues with their devices and software. Entrepreneurs can offer subscription-based plans and on-demand assistance, leveraging remote tools and expertise.

Starting a remote tech support business requires a range of tools and resources to effectively provide technical assistance to clients from a distance. Here's a comprehensive list of the essential tools you'll need:

1. Communication Tools
   a. VoIP Phone System: For handling client calls over the internet.
   Examples: Zoom Phone, RingCentral, VoIP.ms.

b. Video Conferencing Software: For video calls and remote support sessions.
   <u>Examples:</u> Zoom, Microsoft Teams, Google Meet.
   c. Messaging and Collaboration Tools: For chat-based communication and team collaboration.
   <u>Examples:</u> Slack, Microsoft Teams, Discord.

2. Remote Access and Support Tools

   a. Remote Desktop Software: For accessing and controlling client computers remotely.
   <u>Examples:</u> TeamViewer, AnyDesk, RemotePC, LogMeIn.
   b. Remote Support Tools: For providing live support and troubleshooting.
   <u>Examples:</u> Zoho Assist, Splashtop, ConnectWise Control.
   c. Screen Sharing Software: For demonstrating solutions and guiding clients through troubleshooting.
   <u>Examples:</u> Join.me, Screenleap.

3. Ticketing and Management Tools

   a. Help Desk Software: For managing support requests and tracking tickets.
   <u>Examples:</u> Zendesk, Freshdesk, ServiceNow.
   b. Customer Relationship Management (CRM) Software: For managing client information and interactions.
   <u>Examples:</u> HubSpot CRM, Salesforce, Zoho CRM.

c. Task Management Tools: For assigning and tracking tasks within your team.
Examples: Asana, Trello, Monday.com.

4. Security Tools
a. Antivirus and Anti-Malware Software: For protecting client systems from threats.
Examples: Norton, Bitdefender, Malwarebytes.
b. VPN Software: For secure and encrypted access to client systems.
Examples: NordVPN, ExpressVPN, CyberGhost.
c. Security Software for Remote Access: For securing remote sessions and data transfers.
Examples: Duo Security, LastPass, 1Password.

5. Diagnostic and Troubleshooting Tools
a. System Diagnostic Tools: For analyzing and diagnosing system issues.
Examples: CCleaner, CPU-Z, HWMonitor.
b. Network Diagnostic Tools: For troubleshooting network-related problems.
Examples: PingPlotter, Wireshark, NetSpot.
c. Backup and Recovery Tools: For assisting with data backup and recovery.
Examples: Acronis True Image, EaseUS Todo Backup.

6. Knowledge Management Tools
a. Knowledge Base Software: For creating and maintaining a repository of solutions and FAQs.

Examples: Confluence, Helpjuice, Document360.
b. Documentation Tools: For creating and managing support documents and guides.
Examples: Google Docs, Microsoft Word, Notion.

7. Marketing and Sales Tools
a. Website and Landing Page Builders: For creating a professional website and landing pages.
Examples: WordPress, Wix, Squarespace.
b. Email Marketing Software: For sending marketing emails and managing client communications.
Examples: Mailchimp, Sendinblue, Constant Contact.
c. Analytics Tools: For tracking website performance and marketing efforts.
Examples: Google Analytics, Hotjar.

8. Administrative Tools
a. Time Tracking Software: For tracking time spent on support tasks and billing clients.
Examples: Toggl, Harvest.
b. Business Insurance: To cover liabilities and protect your business.

9. Workspace Setup
a. Computer and Hardware: Essential equipment for performing tech support.
Examples: High-performance computer, dual monitors, headset.

b. Ergonomic Furniture: To ensure a comfortable and productive workspace.
      Examples: Ergonomic chair, adjustable desk.
   c. High-Speed Internet Connection: Reliable and fast internet is crucial for remote support.

10. Miscellaneous Tools
   a. Training and Certification: For maintaining and improving technical skills.
      Examples: Online courses, certifications like CompTIA A+.
   b. Professional Associations: For networking and professional development.
      Examples: Information Technology Services Management (ITSM) organizations, local tech groups.

By equipping yourself with these tools and resources, you'll be well-prepared to start and run a successful remote tech support business. Focus on delivering exceptional service, maintaining security, and effectively managing client relationships to build a strong reputation and grow your business.

18. Virtual Event Planning

Virtual event planning services cater to organizations transitioning to online formats for conferences, trade shows, and networking events. Entrepreneurs with event management experience can offer comprehensive solutions, including platform selection, content creation, and technical support.

Starting a virtual event planning business involves using various tools to manage event logistics, coordinate with clients and vendors, and deliver engaging online experiences. Here's a comprehensive list of the essential tools and resources you'll need:

1. **Event Planning and Management Tools**
    a. Event Management Software: For planning, organizing, and managing events.
       Examples: Eventbrite, Cvent, Bizzabo.
    b. Project Management Tools: For tracking tasks, deadlines, and team collaboration.
       Examples: Asana, Trello, Monday.com, ClickUp.
    c. Budget Management Software: For managing and tracking event budgets.
       Examples: Microsoft Excel, Google Sheets, QuickBooks.

2. **Virtual Event Platforms**
    a. Video Conferencing Software: For hosting live events, webinars, and meetings.

Examples: Zoom, Microsoft Teams, Google Meet, Cisco Webex.
   b. Virtual Event Platforms: Specialized platforms for creating immersive virtual events.
   Examples: Hopin, vFairs, Run The World, Brella.
   c. Webinar Software: For hosting webinars and interactive sessions.
   Examples: WebinarJam, GoToWebinar, Demio.

3. **Communication and Collaboration Tools**
   a. Messaging and Collaboration Tools: For internal communication and client coordination.
   Examples: Slack, Microsoft Teams, Discord.
   b. Email Marketing Software: For sending event invitations, updates, and follow-ups.
   Examples: Mailchimp, Sendinblue, Constant Contact.
   c. Social Media Management Tools: For promoting events and engaging with attendees on social media.
   Examples: Hootsuite, Buffer, Later.

4. **Design and Branding Tools**
   a. Graphic Design Software: For creating event branding materials, social media posts, and marketing assets.
   Examples: Adobe Creative Suite (Photoshop, Illustrator), Canva.

b. Video Editing Software: For editing promotional videos, event highlights, and recorded content.
Examples: Adobe Premiere Pro, Final Cut Pro, DaVinci Resolve.

5. Registration and Ticketing Tools
a. Registration Software: For managing attendee registrations and ticketing.
Examples: Eventbrite, Ticket Tailor, RegFox.
b. Payment Processing Tools: For handling payments for event tickets and services.
Examples: PayPal, Stripe, Square.

6. Audience Engagement Tools
a. Polling and Survey Tools: For collecting feedback and engaging with attendees.
Examples: Slido, Mentimeter, SurveyMonkey.
b. Live Chat Tools: For real-time communication with event attendees.
Examples: Chatroll, Tawk.to, Intercom.
c. Gamification Tools: For adding interactive elements and games to virtual events.
Examples: Kahoot!, Quizizz, EventMobi.

7. Analytics and Reporting Tools
a. Analytics Platforms: For tracking event performance, attendee engagement, and metrics.
Examples: Google Analytics, Eventbrite Analytics, Mixpanel.

b. Reporting Tools: For generating detailed reports on event outcomes and attendee behavior.
Examples: Microsoft Power BI, Tableau.

8. Administrative and Financial Tools
   a. Time Tracking Software: For tracking time spent on planning and executing events.
   Examples: Toggl, Harvest.
   b. Contract and Proposal Management: For creating and managing client contracts and proposals.
   Examples: PandaDoc, Proposify.

9. Workspace and Equipment
   a. Computer and Hardware: Essential equipment for managing events and virtual meetings.
   Examples: High-performance computer, webcam, microphone.
   b. Ergonomic Furniture: To ensure a comfortable and productive workspace.
   Examples: Ergonomic chair, adjustable desk.
   c. High-Speed Internet Connection: Reliable internet is crucial for smooth virtual event execution.

10. Miscellaneous Tools
   a. Training and Certification: For maintaining and improving event planning skills.
   Examples: Online courses, certifications from organizations like Meeting Professionals International (MPI).

   b. **Professional Associations:** For networking and professional development.
   <u>Examples:</u> International Live Events Association (ILEA), Event Industry Council (EIC).

By equipping yourself with these tools and setting up an efficient workspace, you'll be well-prepared to start and run a successful virtual event planning business. Focus on delivering high-quality, engaging virtual events and building strong client relationships to grow your business.

19. E-book Publishing

E-book publishing offers aspiring authors a platform to share their works with global audiences, bypassing traditional publishing barriers. Entrepreneurs can provide editorial, design, and distribution services to self-published authors, earning revenue through royalties and fees. Starting an eBook publishing business involves a variety of tools and resources for creating, publishing, and marketing eBooks. Here's a comprehensive list of the essential tools and equipment you'll need:

1. Writing and Editing Tools
   a. **Word Processing Software:** For writing and formatting your eBooks.
   <u>Examples</u>: Microsoft Word, Google Docs, Apple Pages.

b. Writing Software: Specialized software for writing and organizing content.
      Examples: Scrivener, Ulysses, yWriter.
   c. Editing and Proofreading Tools: For grammar checking and style suggestions.
      Examples: Grammarly, ProWritingAid, Hemingway Editor.
   d. Professional Editing Services: For additional editing, proofreading, and quality assurance.
      Examples: Fiverr, Upwork (for freelance editors).

2. **eBook Formatting and Design Tools**
   a. eBook Formatting Software: For converting manuscripts into eBook formats like EPUB and MOBI.
      Examples: Calibre, Adobe InDesign, Scrivener (for formatting).
   b. eBook Conversion Tools: For converting eBooks to different formats.
      Examples: Kindle Create, Sigil.
   c. Cover Design Software: For designing eye-catching eBook covers.
      Examples: Adobe Photoshop, Canva, GIMP.

3. **Publishing Platforms**
   a. Self-Publishing Platforms: For publishing and distributing your eBooks.
      Examples: Amazon Kindle Direct Publishing (KDP), Apple Books, Barnes & Noble Press, Kobo Writing Life.
   b. Aggregators: For distributing eBooks to multiple retailers.

Examples: Smashwords, Draft2Digital, PublishDrive.

4. Marketing and Promotion Tools

a. Website Builders: For creating a professional author or publishing website.
Examples: WordPress, Wix, Squarespace.

b. Email Marketing Software: For building an email list and sending newsletters and promotions.
Examples: Mailchimp, ConvertKit, Sendinblue.

c. Social Media Management Tools: For managing and scheduling social media posts.
Examples: Hootsuite, Buffer, Later.

d. Book Promotion and Review Sites: For promoting your eBooks and gaining reviews.
Examples: Goodreads, BookBub, NetGalley.

5. Analytics and Tracking Tools

a. Analytics Platforms: For tracking eBook sales, website traffic, and marketing performance.
Examples: Google Analytics, KDP Reports, Book Report.

b. Sales Tracking Tools: For monitoring eBook sales across different platforms.
Examples: Sales data from KDP, Smashwords, or your chosen distributor.

6. **Administrative Tools**
   a. Contract and Agreement Templates: For managing author agreements, publishing contracts, and royalty arrangements.
   Examples: PandaDoc, LegalZoom, Rocket Lawyer.

7. **Workspace and Equipment**
   a. Computer and Software: Essential tools for writing, designing, and managing eBooks.
   Examples: High-performance computer, relevant software.
   b. Ergonomic Furniture: To ensure a comfortable working environment.
   Examples: Ergonomic chair, adjustable desk.
   c. High-Speed Internet Connection: For efficient uploading, downloading, and online communications.

8. **Miscellaneous Tools**
   a. Research Tools: For researching content, trends, and market demands.
   Examples: Google Scholar, JSTOR, industry blogs.
   b. Professional Associations: For networking and professional development.
   Examples: Independent Book Publishers Association (IBPA), Authors Guild.
   c. Training and Courses: For learning about eBook publishing, marketing, and business management.
   Examples: Online courses on Udemy, Coursera, LinkedIn Learning.

By equipping yourself with these tools and setting up a structured workflow, you'll be well-prepared to start and run a successful eBook publishing business. Focus on producing high-quality content, effective marketing strategies, and building strong relationships with readers and industry professionals.

20. Language Translation Services

Language translation services facilitate communication and collaboration across cultures and languages. Entrepreneurs with fluency in multiple languages can offer translation, localization, and interpretation services to businesses and individuals operating in diverse markets.

Starting a language translation service business requires a blend of tools for translation, project management, client communication, and business operations. Here's a detailed list of essential tools and resources you'll need:

1. Translation Tools
- a. Translation Software (CAT Tools): Computer-Assisted Translation (CAT) tools help manage translation projects and ensure consistency.
  Examples: SDL Trados Studio, MemoQ, Wordfast, MateCat.
- b. Machine Translation Tools: Automated tools for translating text, useful for initial drafts or specific use cases.
  Examples: Google Translate, DeepL, Microsoft Translator.
- c. Dictionary and Thesaurus: For finding accurate translations and understanding nuances in different languages.
  Examples: Oxford Dictionaries, Collins Dictionary.

d. Language Reference Tools: Resources for understanding language grammar, usage, and idioms.
Examples: Grammarly, LanguageTool, Linguee.

2. Project Management Tools

a. Project Management Software: For managing translation projects, deadlines, and tasks.
Examples: Asana, Trello, Monday.com, ClickUp.

b. Task Management Tools: For organizing individual tasks and tracking progress.
Examples: Todoist, Wunderlist, Microsoft To Do.

3. Communication and Collaboration Tools

a. Communication Platforms. For client and team communication.
Examples: Zoom, Microsoft Teams, Slack.

b. File Sharing and Collaboration Tools: For sharing documents and collaborating on translations.
Examples: Google Drive, Dropbox, OneDrive.

c. Email Marketing and Communication Tools: For sending proposals, updates, and newsletters.
Examples: Mailchimp, Sendinblue, Constant Contact.

4. **Client and Invoice Management Tools**
   a. Customer Relationship Management (CRM) Software: For managing client interactions, tracking leads, and maintaining client information.
   <u>Examples:</u> HubSpot CRM, Salesforce, Zoho CRM.
   b. Invoicing and Accounting Software: For creating invoices, tracking payments, and managing finances.
   <u>Examples:</u> QuickBooks, FreshBooks, Xero.
   c. Proposal and Contract Management: For creating and managing client proposals and contracts.
   <u>Examples:</u> PandaDoc, Proposify, HelloSign.

5. **Website and Online Presence Tools**
   a. Website Builder: For creating a professional website to showcase your services.
   <u>Examples:</u> WordPress, Wix, Squarespace.
   b. SEO Tools: For optimizing your website and increasing visibility.
   <u>Examples:</u> Google Analytics, SEMrush, Moz.
   c. Social Media Management Tools: For managing and scheduling posts to promote your services.
   <u>Examples:</u> Hootsuite, Buffer, Later.

6. **Professional Development Tools**
   a. Training and Certification: For improving translation skills and obtaining certifications.

Examples: ATA Certification, CIOL Diploma in Translation, online courses on Udemy or Coursera.
   b. Industry Associations: For networking and professional growth.
      Examples: American Translators Association (ATA), International Federation of Translators (FIT).

7. Administrative Tools
   a. Time Tracking Software: For tracking time spent on projects and billing clients.
      Examples: Toggl, Harvest, Time Doctor.
   b. Legal and Compliance Tools: For managing legal aspects of your business.
      Examples: LegalZoom, Rocket Lawyer (for contracts, legal advice).
   c. Business Insurance: To protect your business from potential risks and liabilities.

8. Miscellaneous Tools
   a. Translation Memory (TM) Systems: To store previously translated segments for consistency and efficiency.
      Examples: SDL Trados Studio, MemoQ, Wordfast.
   b. Glossaries and Terminology Management: For maintaining consistency in technical or specialized translations.
      Examples: SDL MultiTerm, TermBase.

By assembling these tools and resources, you'll be well-equipped to launch and manage a successful language translation service business. Focus on delivering high-quality translations, maintaining strong client relationships, and leveraging effective marketing strategies to grow your business.

21. Online Tutoring

Online tutoring services cater to students seeking academic support and enrichment outside traditional classroom settings. Entrepreneurs with expertise in specific subjects or standardized tests can offer personalized lessons and coaching sessions, leveraging digital platforms for delivery. Starting an online tutoring business involves using various tools to facilitate effective teaching, manage your business operations, and interact with students. Here's a detailed list of the essential tools and resources you'll need:

1. Online Teaching Tools
   a. Video Conferencing Software: For live tutoring sessions and face-to-face interactions.
   Examples: Zoom, Microsoft Teams, Google Meet, Cisco Webex.
   b. Virtual Whiteboard: For interactive teaching and drawing diagrams.
   Examples: Miro, Ziteboard, Jamboard, Whiteboard.fi.
   c. Learning Management System (LMS): For organizing course materials, assignments, and tracking student progress.
   Examples: Moodle, Teachable, Thinkific, Kajabi.
   d. Screen Sharing Software: For sharing your screen with students during sessions.

Examples: Zoom (built-in feature), Microsoft Teams, AnyDesk.
   e. Document Sharing and Collaboration: For sharing and collaborating on documents and assignments.
      Examples: Google Drive, Dropbox, Microsoft OneDrive.

2. **Tutoring Management Tools**
   a. Scheduling Software: For scheduling tutoring sessions and managing appointments.
      Examples: Calendly, Acuity Scheduling, SimplyBook.me.
   b. Payment Processing Tools: For handling payments and managing transactions.
      Examples: PayPal, Stripe, Square.
   c. Client Management Software: For managing student information, communication, and progress.
      Examples: HubSpot CRM, Zoho CRM, 17hats.

3. **Marketing and Outreach Tools**
   a. Website Builder: For creating a professional website to promote your tutoring services.
      Examples: WordPress, Wix, Squarespace.
   b. SEO Tools: For optimizing your website and improving search engine rankings.
      Examples: Google Analytics, SEMrush, Moz.
   c. Social Media Management Tools: For managing social media accounts and scheduling posts.
      Examples: Hootsuite, Buffer, Later.

d. Email Marketing Software: For sending newsletters, promotional emails, and updates.
   Examples: Mailchimp, Sendinblue, ConvertKit.

4. Content Creation Tools
   a. Graphic Design Software: For creating marketing materials, course materials, and visuals.
   Examples: Canva, Adobe Photoshop, Adobe Illustrator.
   b. Video Editing Software: For creating and editing instructional videos and content.
   Examples: Adobe Premiere Pro, Final Cut Pro, Camtasia.
   c. Management System (CMS): For managing and publishing educational content.
   Examples: WordPress, Joomla, Drupal.

5. Educational Resources and Tools
   a. Interactive Learning Tools: For engaging students and enhancing the learning experience.
   Examples: Kahoot!, Quizlet, Nearpod.
   b. Assessment Tools: For creating and administering quizzes, tests, and assessments.
   Examples: Google Forms, Typeform, Quizizz.
   c. Educational Software: For delivering specialized content or practicing skills.

Examples: Duolingo (for language learning), Khan Academy, Coursera.

6. Administrative Tools
   a. Time Tracking Software: For tracking time spent on tutoring and managing schedules.
   Examples: Toggl, Harvest, Time Doctor.
   b. Contract and Agreement Templates: For creating and managing tutoring contracts and agreements.
   Examples: PandaDoc, LegalZoom, DocuSign.

7. Workspace Setup
   a. Computer and Hardware: Essential tools for conducting online tutoring sessions.
   Examples: High-performance computer, webcam, microphone, headset.
   b. Ergonomic Furniture: To ensure a comfortable and productive workspace.
   Examples: Ergonomic chair, adjustable desk.
   c. High-Speed Internet Connection: Reliable internet is crucial for smooth online sessions.

8. Miscellaneous Tools
   a. Professional Development: For staying updated on teaching methods and business practices.
   Examples: Online courses, webinars, professional organizations.
   b. Networking Platforms: For connecting with other educators and potential clients.
   Examples: LinkedIn, Facebook Groups for educators.

By utilizing these tools and setting up a well-organized workflow, you'll be equipped to start and manage a successful online tutoring business. Focus on providing high-quality instruction, maintaining strong client relationships, and effectively marketing your services to attract and retain students.

22. Virtual Fitness Coaching

Virtual fitness coaching services provide personalized workout plans and guidance to individuals pursuing their health and wellness goals. Entrepreneurs can offer remote training sessions, nutritional counseling, and accountability support, leveraging technology to connect with clients worldwide.

Starting a virtual fitness coaching business involves using a variety of tools to deliver workouts, manage clients, handle administrative tasks, and market your services. Here's a comprehensive list of the essential tools and resources you'll need:

1. Fitness Coaching Tools
   a. Video Conferencing Software: For live coaching sessions and virtual group classes.
      Examples: Zoom, Microsoft Teams, Google Meet, Skype.
   b. Workout Programming Software: For creating and managing workout plans and routines.
      Examples: Trainerize, My PT Hub, FitBot, TrueCoach.
   c. Fitness Tracking Apps: For tracking client progress and fitness metrics.
      Examples: MyFitnessPal, Strava, Fitbit.
   d. Virtual Fitness Platforms: Specialized platforms for delivering virtual fitness classes and coaching.
      Examples: Mindbody, ClassPass, Glofox.

2. **Client Management Tools**
   a. Scheduling Software: For managing appointments, booking sessions, and scheduling classes.
      Examples: Calendly, Acuity Scheduling, SimplyBook.me
   b. Client Management and CRM Software: For tracking client interactions, progress, and communication.
      Examples: HubSpot CRM, Zoho CRM, 17hats, Notion.ai
   c. Payment Processing Tools: For handling payments and managing transactions.
      Examples: PayPal, Stripe, Square.
3. **Communication Tools**
   a. Email Marketing Software:- For sending newsletters, workout updates, and promotional materials.
      Examples: Mailchimp, ConvertKit, Sendinblue.
   b. Messaging Apps: For direct communication with clients.
      Examples: WhatsApp, Telegram, Signal.
   c. Social Media Management Tools: For managing and scheduling posts to engage with clients and promote your services.
      Examples: Hootsuite, Buffer, Later.
4. **Content Creation Tools**
   a. Video Editing Software: For creating and editing workout videos, tutorials, and promotional content.

Examples: Adobe Premiere Pro, Final Cut Pro, Camtasia, Capcut
  b. Graphic Design Software: For designing marketing materials, social media posts, and workout guides.
  Examples: Canva, Adobe Photoshop, Adobe Illustrator.
  c. Website Builder: For creating a professional website to promote your fitness coaching business.
  Examples: WordPress, Wix, Squarespace, Weebly

5. **Administrative Tools**
   a. Time Tracking Software: For tracking time spent on sessions and administrative tasks.
   Examples: Toggl, Harvest, Time Doctor.
   b. Contract and Agreement Templates: For creating and managing client contracts and agreements.
   Examples: PandaDoc, LegalZoom, DocuSign.

6. **Fitness and Wellness Resources**
   a. Nutrition and Meal Planning Tools: For providing clients with meal plans and dietary guidance.
   Examples: MyFitnessPal, EatLove, Cronometer.
   b. Wellness Apps: For supporting holistic health, including sleep, stress management, and mindfulness.
   Examples: Calm, Headspace, Insight Timer.

7. Marketing and Branding Tools
   a. SEO Tools: For optimizing your website and improving search engine rankings.
      Examples: Google Analytics, SEMrush, Moz.
   b. Social Proof and Review Platforms: For gathering and showcasing client testimonials and reviews.
      Examples: Trustpilot, Google Reviews, Yelp.
   c. Online Advertising Platforms: For running targeted ads to attract new clients.
      Examples: Facebook Ads, Google Ads, Instagram Ads.

8. Workspace Setup
   a. Computer and Hardware: Essential tools for conducting virtual coaching and managing your business.
      Examples: High-performance computer, webcam, microphone, headset.
   b. Ergonomic Furniture: To ensure a comfortable and productive workspace.
      Examples: Ergonomic chair, adjustable desk.
   c. High-Speed Internet Connection: Reliable internet is crucial for smooth virtual coaching sessions.

9. Miscellaneous Tools
   a. Professional Development: For staying updated on fitness trends, certifications, and coaching techniques.
      Examples: Online courses, certifications from organizations like NASM or ACE.

b. Networking Platforms: For connecting with other fitness professionals and potential clients.
   Examples: LinkedIn, Facebook Groups for fitness professionals.

By integrating these tools and setting up a streamlined workflow, you'll be well-equipped to start and manage a successful virtual fitness coaching business. Focus on delivering high-quality coaching, maintaining strong client relationships, and effectively marketing your services to grow your business.

23. Podcast Production Services

Podcast production services cater to businesses and individuals looking to create high-quality audio content for marketing and entertainment purposes. Entrepreneurs with audio engineering and storytelling skills can offer editing, mixing, and distribution services to clients across industries.

Starting a podcast production services business involves a variety of tools and resources to handle recording, editing, publishing, and marketing podcasts. Here's a comprehensive list of the essential tools you'll need:

1. Recording Equipment
   a. Microphone: High-quality microphones for clear audio recording.
   <u>Examples:</u> Shure SM7B, Audio-Technica AT2020, Rode NT1-A.
   b. Headphones: For monitoring audio quality during recording and editing.
   <u>Examples:</u> Audio-Technica ATH-M50x, Beyerdynamic DT 770 Pro, Sennheiser HD280 Pro.
   c. Audio Interface: Connects microphones and other audio equipment to your computer.
   <u>Examples:</u> Focusrite Scarlett 2i2, PreSonus AudioBox, Behringer UMC22.
   d. Pop Filter: Reduces plosive sounds and improves audio quality.
   <u>Examples:</u> Aokeo Professional Pop Filter, Heil PR-40 Pop Filter.

e. Shock Mount and Boom Arm: Minimizes vibrations and positions the microphone properly.
     Examples: Heil PR-40 Shock Mount, Rode PSA1 Boom Arm.
  f. Acoustic Treatment: Enhances recording environment by reducing echo and background noise.
     Examples: Acoustic foam panels, soundproofing curtains.

2. **Recording and Editing Software**
   a. Digital Audio Workstation (DAW): Software for recording, editing, and mixing audio.
      Examples: Adobe Audition, Audacity, GarageBand, Reaper.
   b. Audio Editing Plugins: Additional tools for enhancing audio quality.
      Examples: iZotope RX, Waves Plugins, FabFilter Pro-Q.
   c. Remote Recording Software: For recording interviews with guests remotely.
      Examples: Riverside.fm, SquadCast, Zencastr.

3. **Publishing and Distribution Tools**
   a. Podcast Hosting Platforms: For storing and distributing podcast episodes.
      Examples: Libsyn, Podbean, Anchor, Buzzsprout.
   b. Really Simple Syndication (RSS) Feed Generator: Generates an RSS feed for submitting your podcast to directories.

Examples: Provided by hosting platforms like Podbean or Libsyn.
   c. Podcast Directory Submissions: For distributing your podcast to various platforms.
      Examples: Apple Podcasts, Spotify, Google Podcasts, Stitcher.

4. Marketing and Promotion Tools
   a. Social Media Management Tools: For managing social media accounts and scheduling posts.
      Examples: Hootsuite, Buffer, Later.
   b. Graphic Design Software: For creating cover art, promotional materials, and social media graphics.
      Examples: Canva, Adobe Photoshop, Adobe Illustrator.
   c. Email Marketing Software: For sending newsletters, updates, and promotional emails.
      Examples: Mailchimp, ConvertKit, Sendinblue.

5. Administrative and Project Management Tools
   a. Project Management Software: For organizing tasks, deadlines, and team collaboration.
      Examples: Asana, Trello, Monday.com, ClickUp.
   b. Client Management Software: For managing client relationships and tracking interactions.

Examples: HubSpot CRM, Zoho CRM, 17hats.
   c. Invoicing and Accounting Software: For managing finances, invoicing clients, and tracking expenses.
   Examples: QuickBooks, FreshBooks, Xero.

6. **Professional Development and Resources**
   a. Training and Certification: For improving podcast production skills and staying updated on industry trends.
   Examples: Online courses on platforms like Udemy, Coursera, or LinkedIn Learning.
   b. Industry Associations: For networking and professional development.
   Examples: Podcast Movement, Podcaster's Society.

7. **Workspace Setup**
   a. Computer and Hardware: Essential tools for recording, editing, and managing podcasts.
   Examples: High-performance computer, external hard drives for storage.
   b. Ergonomic Furniture: To ensure a comfortable and productive workspace.
   Examples: Ergonomic chair, adjustable desk.
   c. High-Speed Internet Connection: Reliable internet is crucial for uploading episodes and managing online content.

8. **Miscellaneous Tools**
   a. Backup and Storage Solutions: For securing and backing up podcast files and recordings.

  <u>Examples:</u> External hard drives, cloud storage services like Google Drive or Dropbox.
 b. Legal and Compliance Tools: For managing legal aspects, such as contracts and rights management.
  <u>Examples:</u> LegalZoom, Rocket Lawyer (for contracts and legal advice).

By integrating these tools and resources into your workflow, you'll be well-prepared to start and manage a successful podcast production services business. Focus on delivering high-quality audio, maintaining strong client relationships, and effectively marketing your services to attract and retain clients.

24. Mobile Car Wash

Mobile car wash services offer convenience and flexibility to vehicle owners seeking professional cleaning solutions. Entrepreneurs can invest in eco-friendly equipment and water-efficient practices, targeting residential and commercial customers in urban and suburban areas.

Starting a mobile car wash business involves a variety of tools and equipment to provide efficient and high-quality car washing services at clients' locations. Here's a comprehensive list of the essential tools and resources you'll need:

1. Vehicle and Equipment
   a. Service Vehicle: A reliable vehicle to transport all your equipment and supplies.
   Examples: Cargo van, truck, or SUV are preferred but can work out of any size car
   b. Water Tank: To carry water for washing vehicles when access to a water source when one is not available.
   Examples: 100-200 gallon water tank, depending on service needs.
   c. Pressure Washer: For effectively cleaning vehicle surfaces.
   Examples: Gas-powered pressure washer with adjustable pressure settings, or cordless pressure washer (battery operated).
   d. Generator: (optional) To power your equipment if there is no available power source.

Examples: Portable generator, inverter generator.
   e. Hoses and Nozzles: For water delivery and rinsing.
      Examples: High-pressure hose, various nozzles for different spray patterns.

2. Cleaning Supplies and Chemicals
   a. Car Wash Soap: Specially formulated soap for washing vehicles.
      Examples: pH-balanced car wash soap, biodegradable options.
   b. Detailer's Clay: For removing contaminants from the vehicle's surface before waxing.
      Examples: Clay bars or clay mitts.
   c. Wax and Sealants: To protect and shine the vehicle's paint.
      Examples: Carnauba wax, synthetic sealants.
   d. Tire and Wheel Cleaner: For cleaning tires and wheels effectively.
      Examples: Specialized tire and wheel cleaner solutions.
   e. Glass Cleaner: For streak-free cleaning of windows and mirrors.
      Examples: Ammonia-free glass cleaner or vinegar-based solutions
   f. Microfiber Towels: For drying and polishing without scratching surfaces.
   g. Sponges and Wash Mitts: For washing vehicle surfaces.

Examples: Microfiber wash mitts, soft sponges.

3. Safety and Operational Gear
   a. Safety Gear: For personal protection during car washing.
      Examples: Gloves, safety glasses, knee pads.
   b. First Aid Kit: For handling any minor injuries or accidents.
      Examples: Basic first aid supplies like bandages, antiseptics, and ointments.
   c. Portable Lighting: For working in low-light conditions or early morning/late evening jobs. Can use an inverter to connect to you battery to run if needed.
      Examples: LED work lights, portable floodlights.

4. Administrative and Customer Management Tools
   a. Scheduling Software: For managing appointments and client scheduling.
      Examples: Calendly, Acuity Scheduling, SimplyBook.me.
   b. Payment Processing Tools: For handling payments and transactions.
      Examples: Square, PayPal, Stripe.
   c. CRM Software: For managing client information and interactions.
      Examples: HubSpot CRM, Zoho CRM.
   d. Invoicing and Accounting Software: For invoicing clients and managing finances.

Examples: QuickBooks, FreshBooks, Xero.

5. Marketing and Branding Tools

a. Website Builder: For creating a professional website to promote your services.
Examples: WordPress, Wix, Squarespace.

b. Social Media Management Tools: For managing and scheduling posts to engage with customers and promote services.
Examples: Hootsuite, Buffer, Later.

c. Graphic Design Software: For creating promotional materials and branding.
Examples: Canva, Adobe Photoshop, Adobe Illustrator.

d. Business Cards and Flyers: For offline marketing and distributing information.
Examples: Printed business cards, flyers, and brochures.

6. Operational and Miscellaneous Tools

a. Waterless Car Wash Products: For cleaning vehicles when water access is limited.
Examples: Waterless wash solutions, quick detailers.

b. Portable Vacuum Cleaner: For interior cleaning and detailing.
Examples: Handheld vacuum, wet/dry vacuum.

c. Storage Solutions: For organizing and storing equipment and supplies in your vehicle.
Examples: Toolboxes, storage bins, cargo organizers.

d. Vehicle Maintenance: To keep your service vehicle in good working condition.
   <u>Examples</u>: Regular servicing and maintenance of the vehicle.

7. Legal and Compliance Tools
   a. Business Insurance: To protect against liabilities and damages.
   <u>Examples</u>: General liability insurance, commercial vehicle insurance.
   b. Licensing and Permits: Ensure compliance with local regulations and obtain necessary licenses.
   <u>Examples</u>: Business license, any specific permits for operating a mobile car wash.

By equipping yourself with these tools and setting up a well-organized operation, you'll be well-prepared to start and run a successful mobile car wash business. Focus on delivering excellent service, maintaining strong customer relationships, and effectively marketing your services to attract and retain clients.

25. Pet Sitting/Walking

Pet sitting/walking services cater to pet owners seeking reliable and loving care for their animals while they are away. Entrepreneurs can offer in-home visits or overnight stays, ensuring pets are well-fed, entertained, and safe in their familiar environment. Launching a pet-sitting/walking business requires a mix of tools and resources to provide high-quality care for pets. Here's a comprehensive list of essentials you'll need:

1. Pet Care Tools

   a. **Leashes, Collars, and Harnesses**: For walking and handling pets safely.
   Examples: Adjustable leashes, harnesses for different breeds, retractable leashes.
   b. **Food and Water Bowls**: Portable and hygienic containers for feeding pets. Collapsable bowls are useful when traveling.
   c. **Pet Toys and Enrichment**: For keeping pets entertained and mentally stimulated.
   Examples: Chew toys, puzzle feeders, cat wands.
   d. **Waste Bags and Scoopers**: For cleaning up after pets during walks or in the yard.
   Examples: Biodegradable waste bags, litter scoopers.
   e. **Litter Boxes and Cleaning Supplies**: For cat care during visits.
   Examples: Covered litter boxes, clumping litter, odor eliminators.

2. **Safety and Comfort Tools**
   a. **Pet Restraints and Safety Gates**: To manage pets indoors and outdoors safely.
      <u>Examples:</u> Baby gates, playpens for small animals, pet barriers.
   b. **First Aid Kit for Pets**: Essential for addressing minor injuries or emergencies.
      <u>Examples:</u> Pet-safe antiseptics, gauze, bandages, tweezers.
   c. **Transport Carriers and Crates**: For safe transportation when needed.
      <u>Examples:</u> Soft-sided carriers, hard plastic crates, travel crates.
3. **Cleaning and Sanitizing Supplies**
   a. **Pet-Safe Cleaning Products**: For maintaining cleanliness in the pet's environment.
      <u>Examples:</u> Disinfectants, odor removers, pet-safe cleaning wipes.
   b. **Grooming Wipes and Brushes**: To keep pets clean between baths.
      <u>Examples:</u> Pet grooming wipes, de-shedding brushes, slicker brushes.
   c. **Waste Disposal Tools**: To manage waste efficiently.
      <u>Examples:</u> Trash bins with liners, poop bag holders.
4. **Administrative and Client Management Tools**
   a. **Scheduling Software**: For managing appointments and tracking visits.
      <u>Examples:</u> Time To Pet, Rover, Pet Sitter Plus.

- b. **Client and Pet Management Software**: For tracking client details, pet profiles, and care instructions.
  <u>Examples</u>: Pet sitting CRM, Scout, Precise Petcare.
- c. **Payment Processing Tools**: For handling payments and invoices.
  <u>Examples</u>: Venmo, Square, PayPal.
- d. **Invoicing and Accounting Software**: To manage finances and billing clients.
  <u>Examples</u>: QuickBooks, FreshBooks.

5. Marketing and Branding Tools

- a. **Website Builder**: To create a professional website for promoting services.
  <u>Examples</u>: Squarespace, Wix, Weebly.
- b. **Social Media Tools**: For managing social media profiles and posting pet care tips.
  <u>Examples</u>: Hootsuite, Buffer, Later.
- c. **Business Cards and Flyers**: To distribute information about your services.
  <u>Examples</u>: VistaPrint, Canva for creating marketing materials.

6. Workspace Setup

- a. **Pet Sitting Bag**: A dedicated bag to carry all necessary supplies during visits.
  <u>Examples</u>: Large, multi-pocket bags for organizing pet care items.
- b. **Tablet or Smartphone**: To manage appointments, communicate with clients, and access pet care apps.

c. **Reliable Transportation**: For getting to clients' homes and transporting pets if needed.

7. Legal and Compliance Tools

a. **Pet Sitting Insurance**: To protect against liabilities and accidents.
   Examples: Pet sitting insurance, general liability insurance.
b. **Licensing and Permits**: Ensure compliance with local regulations for pet care.
   Examples: Business licenses, certifications from pet-sitting organizations.

8. Training and Referral Marketing

   a. **Pet Care Certification Courses**: For gaining expertise in pet care and improving service quality.
   b. Examples: National Association of Professional Pet Sitters (NAPPS), Pet First Aid courses.
   c. **Networking and Referrals**: Join professional networks and local groups to find clients.
   Examples: LinkedIn, pet-sitting associations, neighborhood apps like Nextdoor.

These are helpful tools and resources that will get you ready to start and run a successful pet sitting business. Focus on providing exceptional care, maintaining a safe and clean environment, and building relationships with both pets and their owners to grow your client base.

26. House Cleaning

House cleaning services provide busy individuals and families with professional cleaning solutions for their homes. Entrepreneurs can offer customizable cleaning plans and eco-friendly products, targeting residential clients in their local communities.

Starting a house cleaning business requires a range of tools and supplies to ensure you can provide efficient and high-quality cleaning services. Here's a comprehensive list of the essential tools and resources you'll need:

1. Cleaning Supplies and Equipment
    a. Vacuum Cleaner: For cleaning carpets and upholstery.
    <u>Examples:</u> Upright vacuum, canister vacuum, cordless vacuum.
    b. Mops and Buckets: For cleaning floors.
    <u>Examples</u>: Wet mops, microfiber mops, bucket with wringer.
    c. Brooms and Dustpans: For sweeping floors and collecting dust and debris.
    <u>Examples:</u> Lobby broom, angle broom, dustpan with handle.
    d. Cleaning Cloths and Rags: For dusting and wiping surfaces.
    <u>Examples:</u> Microfiber cloths, cotton rags.
    e. Scrub Brushes: For scrubbing surfaces and grout.
    <u>Examples:</u> Handheld scrub brushes, long-handled scrub brushes.

- f. Sponges and Scouring Pads: For cleaning dishes, surfaces, and stubborn stains.
  Examples: Non-abrasive sponges, scouring pads.
- g. Cleaning Solutions: For different cleaning tasks and surfaces.
  Examples: All-purpose cleaner, glass cleaner, bathroom cleaner, disinfectant.
- h. Toilet Brushes and Cleaners: For cleaning and maintaining toilets.
  Examples: Toilet brush, toilet bowl cleaner.
- i. Dusters: For removing dust from surfaces.
  Examples: Feather dusters, extendable dusters, microfiber dusters.

2. Safety and Ergonomic Tools
- a. Gloves: For protecting hands during cleaning.
  Examples: Rubber gloves, nitrile gloves.
- b. Safety Glasses (optional): To protect eyes from cleaning chemicals and debris.
- c. Knee Pads: For comfort when cleaning low surfaces or floors.
- d. Personal Protective Equipment (PPE): For safety when handling chemicals.
  Examples: Masks, aprons.

3. Administrative and Client Management Tools
- a. Scheduling Software: For managing cleaning appointments and client schedules.
  Examples: Calendly, Acuity Scheduling, SimplyBook.me.

    b. Client Management Software: For tracking client information and preferences.
   <u>Examples:</u> CRM software, like Zoho CRM, HubSpot CRM.
    c. Payment Processing Tools: For handling payments and transactions.
   <u>Examples:</u> Square, PayPal, Stripe.
    d. Invoicing and Accounting Software: For managing finances and invoicing clients.
   <u>Examples:</u> QuickBooks, FreshBooks, Xero.

4. Marketing and Branding Tools
    a. Website Builder: For creating a professional website to promote your services.
   <u>Examples:</u> WordPress, Wix, Squarespace.
    b. Social Media Management Tools: For managing social media profiles and scheduling posts.
   <u>Examples:</u> Hootsuite, Buffer, Later.
    c. Graphic Design Software: For creating marketing materials and branding.
   <u>Examples:</u> Canva, Adobe Photoshop, Adobe Illustrator.
    d. Business Cards and Flyers: For offline marketing and distributing information about your services.
   <u>Examples:</u> Printed business cards, promotional flyers, and brochures.

5. Operational and Miscellaneous Tools
    a. Storage Solutions: For organizing and storing cleaning supplies.

Examples: Storage bins, caddies, shelving units.

b. Transportation: For transporting cleaning equipment and supplies to clients' homes.
      Examples: Reliable vehicle, possibly with organizational racks or bins.
   c. Uniforms or Workwear: For a professional appearance and easy identification.
      Examples: Branded shirts, aprons.

6. Legal and Compliance Tools
   a. Business Insurance: To protect against liabilities and damages.
      Examples: General liability insurance, workers' compensation insurance.
   b. Licensing and Permits: Ensure compliance with local regulations and obtain necessary licenses.
      Examples: Business license, any specific permits required for cleaning services.

7. Training and Professional Development
   a. Training Materials: For learning best practices and techniques.
      Examples: Online courses, cleaning procedure manuals.
   b. Certifications: To enhance credibility and professional skills.
      Examples: Certifications from cleaning industry organizations or associations.

By equipping yourself with these tools and setting up an efficient operation, you'll be well-prepared to start and manage a successful house cleaning business. Focus on providing high-quality service, maintaining a professional appearance, and effectively marketing your services to attract and retain clients.

27. Gardening Services

Gardening services cater to homeowners and businesses seeking assistance with lawn care, landscaping, and garden maintenance. Entrepreneurs can offer seasonal maintenance plans, plant installation, and design consultations, leveraging their horticultural expertise to create beautiful outdoor spaces.

Starting a gardening service business requires a variety of tools and equipment to handle tasks such as planting, pruning, mowing, and general garden maintenance. Here's a comprehensive list of the essential tools and resources you'll need:

1. Basic Gardening Tools
  a. Shovels and Spades: For digging, turning soil, and planting.
     Examples: Round-point shovel, spade, garden fork.
  b. Rakes: For collecting leaves, debris, and leveling soil.
     Examples: Leaf rake, garden rake, dethatching rake.
  c. Hoes: For weeding and cultivating soil.
     Examples: Garden hoe, draw hoe, stirrup hoe.
  d. Pruning Shears and Loppers: For trimming and shaping plants.

Examples: Bypass pruners, anvil pruners, long-handled loppers.
   e. **Hand Trowels:** For planting and transplanting small plants.
   Examples: Standard hand trowel, transplant trowel.
   f. **Watering Tools:** For watering plants effectively.
   Examples: Watering cans, garden hoses with adjustable nozzles, soaker hoses.
   g. **Garden Gloves:** For protecting hands while working in the garden.
   Examples: Heavy-duty gloves, waterproof gloves.
   h. **Wheelbarrows or Garden Carts (optional):** For transporting soil, plants, and tools.
   Examples: Single-wheel barrow, multi-purpose garden cart.

2. **Lawn Care Tools**
   a. **Lawn Mowers:** For mowing grass and maintaining lawns.
   Examples: Push mowers, riding mowers, zero-turn mowers.
   b. **String Trimmers (Weed Eaters):** For trimming grass and weeds in areas inaccessible to mowers.
   Examples: Gas-powered trimmer, battery-operated trimmer.
   c. **Edgers:** For creating clean lines along lawns, driveways, and flower beds.

Examples: Manual edgers, gas-powered edgers.
  d. Leaf Blowers: For clearing leaves and debris.
  Examples: Backpack leaf blower, handheld leaf blower.

3. Soil and Fertilizer Tools
  a. Soil Test Kits: For testing soil pH and nutrient levels.
  Examples: pH meter, soil testing kit.
  b. Fertilizer Spreaders: For evenly distributing fertilizer.
  Examples: Push spreader, drop spreader.
  c. Composters: For creating compost from organic waste.
  Examples: Compost bins, compost tumblers.

4. Pest and Weed Control Tools
  a. Sprayers: For applying pesticides, herbicides, and fertilizers.
  Examples: Handheld sprayer, backpack sprayer.
  b. Weed Removal Tools: For effectively removing weeds.
  Examples: Weeder tools, weed puller.

5. Safety Gear
  a. Personal Protective Equipment (PPE): For ensuring safety while working.
  Examples: Safety glasses, ear protection, dust masks.
  b. First Aid Kit: For handling minor injuries or emergencies.

Examples: Basic first aid supplies like bandages, antiseptics, ointments.

6. Administrative and Client Management Tools

a. Scheduling Software: For managing appointment s and client schedules.
   Examples: Calendly, Acuity Scheduling, SimplyBook.me.
b. Client Management Software: For tracking client information and garden details.
   Examples: CRM software, like Zoho CRM, HubSpot CRM.
c. Payment Processing Tools: For handling payments and transactions.
   Examples: Square, PayPal, Stripe.
d. Invoicing and Accounting Software: For managing finances and invoicing clients.
   Examples: QuickBooks, FreshBooks, Xero.

7. Marketing and Branding Tools

a. Website Builder: For creating a professional website to promote your services.
   Examples: WordPress, Wix, Squarespace.
b. Social Media Management Tools: For managing social media profiles and scheduling posts.
   Examples: Hootsuite, Buffer, Later.
c. Graphic Design Software: For creating marketing materials and branding.
   Examples: Canva, Adobe Photoshop, Adobe Illustrator.

d. **Business Cards and Flyers:** For offline marketing and distributing information about your services.
      <u>Examples:</u> Printed business cards, promotional flyers, and brochures.

8. **Workspace and Storage Solutions**
   a. **Tool Storage:** For organizing and storing gardening tools and supplies.
      <u>Examples:</u> Tool sheds, storage bins, racks.
   b. **Vehicle:** For transporting tools, equipment, and supplies to job sites.
      <u>Examples:</u> Pickup truck, cargo van.

9. **Legal and Compliance Tools**
   a. **Business Insurance:** To protect against liabilities and damages.
      <u>Examples:</u> General liability insurance, workers' compensation insurance (most states require for 3-5 employees)
   b. **Licensing and Permits:** Ensure compliance with local regulations and obtain necessary licenses.
      <u>Examples:</u> Business license, any specific permits required for gardening services.

10. **Miscellaneous Tools**
    a. **Garden Design Software:** For creating garden layouts and designs.
       <u>Examples:</u> Garden planner tools like SketchUp, Garden Design Software.
    b. **Training and Professional Development:** For improving gardening skills and knowledge.

> Examples: Online courses, workshops, gardening books.

By equipping yourself with these tools and setting up an efficient operation, you'll be well-prepared to start and manage a successful gardening service business. Focus on delivering high-quality service, maintaining a professional appearance, and effectively marketing your services to attract and retain clients.

28. Interior Design Consultancy

Interior design consultancy services help clients transform their living and workspaces into functional and aesthetically pleasing environments. Entrepreneurs can offer design consultations, space planning, and project management services, catering to residential and commercial clients.

Starting an interior design consulting business requires a combination of creative tools, business management tools, and client communication resources. Here's a comprehensive list of the essential tools and resources you'll need:

1. Design and Creativity Tools
- a. Computer and Design Software: For creating design plans, presentations, and visualizations.
  Examples:
  - AutoCAD: For detailed floor plans and elevations.
  - SketchUp: For 3D modeling.

- Revit: For building information modeling (BIM).
- Adobe Creative Suite: For graphic design, including Photoshop, Illustrator, and InDesign.
- 3ds Max: For high-quality 3D renderings.
- Canva: For creating presentations and marketing materials.

b. Digital Drawing Tablet: For sketching and illustrating design concepts.
  <u>Examples:</u> Wacom Intuos, Huion Kamvas.
c. Sample Boards and Mood Boards: For presenting design ideas and color schemes to clients.
  <u>Examples:</u> Digital mood board tools like Milanote or physical sample boards.
d. Color Matching Tools: For selecting and matching colors.
  <u>Examples:</u> Pantone Color Guides, color swatch books.
e. Measuring Tools: For accurate measurements of spaces and furniture.
  <u>Examples:</u> Tape measures, laser distance meters.

2. Business Management Tools

a. Project Management Software: For managing projects, tasks, and deadlines.
  <u>Examples:</u> Asana, Trello, Monday.com.
b. Scheduling Software: For managing appointments and meetings.

Examples: Calendly, Acuity Scheduling, SimplyBook.me.
  c. Client Management Software (CRM): For tracking client information, communications, and project details.
     Examples: HubSpot CRM, Zoho CRM, Salesforce.
  d. Invoicing and Accounting Software: For managing finances and invoicing clients.
     Examples: QuickBooks, FreshBooks, Xero.
  e. File Storage and Sharing: For storing and sharing design files and documents.
     Examples: Google Drive, Dropbox, OneDrive.

3. **Marketing and Branding Tools**
  a. Website Builder: For creating a professional website to showcase your portfolio and services.
     Examples: WordPress, Wix, Squarespace.
  b. Social Media Management Tools: For managing social media profiles and scheduling posts.
     Examples: Hootsuite, Buffer, Later.
  c. Graphic Design Software: For creating marketing materials and branding.
     Examples: Canva, Adobe Photoshop, Adobe Illustrator.
  d. Business Cards and Marketing Materials For offline marketing and distributing information about your services.

Examples: Printed business cards, brochures, flyers.

4. Client Communication Tools
   a. Email Management: For professional communication with clients.
      Examples: Gmail, Outlook, Mailchimp (for newsletters).
   b. Video Conferencing Tools: For virtual meetings and consultations.
      Examples: Zoom, Microsoft Teams, Google Meet.
   c. Proposal and Contract Templates: For formalizing agreements with clients.
      Examples: Templates in Microsoft Word or Google Docs, contract management software like HelloSign.

5. Workspace Setup
   a. Office Furniture: For a comfortable and functional workspace.
      Examples: Desk, ergonomic chair, shelving for samples and materials.
   b. Presentation Tools: For presenting design concepts and ideas.
      Examples: Projector, large display monitor, presentation clicker.

6. Legal and Compliance Tools
   a. Licensing and Permits: Ensure compliance with local regulations and obtain necessary licenses.

Examples: Business license, any specific permits required for interior design consulting.

7. Professional Development
   a. Continuing Education: For staying updated with industry trends and enhancing skills.
      Examples: Online courses, workshops, industry conferences.
   b. Industry Certifications: To enhance credibility and professional skills.
      Examples: Certified Interior Designer (CID), National Council for Interior Design Qualification (NCIDQ).

8. Miscellaneous Tools
   a. Design Samples and Catalogs: For presenting material options and styles to clients.
      Examples: Fabric swatches, flooring samples, catalogues from suppliers.
   b. Reference Materials: For inspiration and design knowledge.
      Examples: Interior design books, magazines, online design resources.

By equipping yourself with these tools and resources, you'll be well-prepared to start and run a successful interior design consulting business. Focus on delivering high-quality, creative solutions, maintaining a professional appearance, and effectively marketing your services to attract and retain clients.

29. Home Staging

Home staging services assist sellers in presenting their properties in the best possible light to attract potential buyers. Entrepreneurs can offer staging consultations, furniture rental, and interior styling services, helping sellers maximize the appeal and value of their homes.

Starting a home staging business involves preparing homes for sale to make them more appealing to potential buyers. This requires a variety of tools and resources to effectively showcase properties and enhance their marketability. Here's a comprehensive list of the essential tools and resources you'll need:

1. **Staging and Furniture Tools**
    a. Furniture and Decor: Essential items to make homes look inviting and stylish.
       <u>Examples:</u>
       - Sofas, chairs, tables, and beds.
       - Rugs, curtains, and bedding.
       - Lamps, artwork, and decorative accessories.
    b. Storage Solutions: For storing and transporting staging furniture and decor.
       <u>Examples:</u> Storage units, moving trucks, shelving units.
    c. Home Staging Accessories: Small items to enhance the visual appeal of a home.
       <u>Examples:</u> Vases, throw pillows, books, plants, and candles.

d. Furniture Rental Services: For acquiring furniture and decor on a temporary basis.
   Examples: Local furniture rental companies, online rental services.

2. **Design and Creativity Tools**
   a. Design Software: For creating staging plans and visualizations.
      Examples:
      - SketchUp: For 3D modeling.
      - AutoCAD: For floor plans.
      - Adobe Photoshop: For image editing.
   b. Color and Fabric Swatches: For selecting colors and materials.
      Examples: Paint color samples, fabric swatches, wallpaper samples.
   c. Measuring Tools: For taking accurate measurements of rooms and furniture.
      Examples: Tape measures, laser distance meters, furniture dimension guides.
   d. Mood Boards and Sample Boards: For presenting design concepts and ideas to clients.
      Examples: Digital tools like Milanote or physical boards.

3. **Logistics and Operations Tools**
   a. Moving and Transport Equipment: For moving furniture and decor in and out of properties.
      Examples: Dollies, furniture sliders, moving blankets.

b. Inventory Management: For keeping track of staging items and their locations.
   Examples: Inventory management software or spreadsheets.
   c. Cleaning Supplies: For preparing homes and ensuring they are spotless before staging.
   Examples: Vacuums, mops, cleaning solutions.
4. **Administrative and Client Management Tools**
   a. Scheduling Software: For managing appointments and staging projects.
   Examples: Calendly, Acuity Scheduling, SimplyBook.me.
   b. Client Management Software (CRM): For tracking client interactions and project details.
   Examples: HubSpot CRM, Zoho CRM, Salesforce.
   c. Invoicing and Accounting Software: For managing finances and generating invoices.
   Examples: QuickBooks, FreshBooks, Xero.
   d. Proposal and Contract Templates: For formalizing agreements with clients.
   Examples: Microsoft Word or Google Docs templates, contract management software.
5. **Marketing and Branding Tools**
   a. Website Builder: For creating a professional online presence.
   Examples: WordPress, Wix, Squarespace.

b. Social Media Management Tools: For managing and scheduling social media posts.
   <u>Examples:</u> Hootsuite, Buffer, Later.
   c. Graphic Design Software: For creating marketing materials and branding.
   <u>Examples:</u> Canva, Adobe Photoshop, Adobe Illustrator.
   d. Business Cards and Marketing Materials: For distributing information about your services.
   <u>Examples:</u> Printed business cards, flyers, brochures.

6. **Client Communication Tools**
   a. Email Management: For professional communication with clients.
   <u>Examples:</u> Gmail, Outlook, Mailchimp (for newsletters).
   b. Video Conferencing Tool: For virtual consultations and presentations.
   <u>Examples:</u> Zoom, Microsoft Teams, Google Meet.
   c. Presentation Tools: For presenting staging plans and ideas.
   <u>Examples:</u> Projector, large display monitor, presentation clicker.

7. **Legal and Compliance Tools**
   a. Licensing and Permits: Ensure compliance with local regulations and obtain necessary licenses.
   <u>Examples:</u> Business license, any specific permits required for staging services.

8. **Workspace Setup**
    a. Office Furniture: For a functional and comfortable work environment.
       Examples: Desk, ergonomic chair, storage solutions.
    b. Design Studio or Workspace: For planning and organizing staging projects.
       Examples: Space for working on design boards, managing inventory.
9. **Professional Development**
    a. Training and Certification: For enhancing skills and credentials.
       Examples: Certifications from home staging organizations or design schools, online courses.
    b. Industry Research: For staying updated on trends and best practices.
       Examples: Industry magazines, online forums, design blogs.

By equipping yourself with these tools and resources, you'll be well-prepared to start and run a successful home staging business. Focus on delivering high-quality, appealing staging solutions, maintaining professional standards, and effectively marketing your services to attract and retain clients.

30. Personal Styling

Personal styling services provide individuals with fashion advice and wardrobe solutions tailored to their preferences and lifestyles. Entrepreneurs can offer in-person or virtual styling sessions, shopping assistance, and closet organization services, helping clients enhance their personal image. Again need marketing platform to find clients.

31. Professional Organizing

Professional organizing services help clients declutter and optimize their living and workspaces for efficiency and productivity. Entrepreneurs can offer hands-on organizing sessions, space planning, and storage solutions, empowering clients to simplify their lives and reduce stress.

Starting a professional organizing business involves helping clients declutter and organize their spaces, which requires a combination of physical tools and organizational resources. Here's a comprehensive list of the essential tools and resources you'll need:

1. Organizational Tools
   a. Storage Containers: For organizing and storing items.
   <u>Examples:</u> Clear bins, stackable containers, drawer organizers.
   b. Labeling Supplies: For identifying and categorizing items.

<u>Examples:</u> Label maker, adhesive labels, labeling pens.
  c. Shelving and Racks: For maximizing vertical storage space.
     <u>Examples:</u> Adjustable shelves, wall-mounted racks, closet organizers.
  d. Baskets and Bins: For grouping similar items together.
     <u>Examples:</u> Wicker baskets, fabric bins, plastic bins.
  e. Drawer Dividers: For keeping items in drawers organized.
     <u>Examples:</u> Adjustable dividers, acrylic organizers.
  f. Hanging Organizers: For storing items in closets and on doors.
     <u>Examples:</u> Over-the-door organizers, hanging shelves, closet hanging organizers.
  g. Document and File Organizers: For managing paperwork and important documents.
     <u>Examples:</u> File folders, document trays, filing cabinets.

2. **Physical Tools**
  a. Measuring Tools: For ensuring that storage solutions fit in the designated spaces.
     <u>Examples:</u> Tape measure, laser distance meter, level.
  b. Cleaning Supplies: For cleaning spaces as part of the organizing process.

Examples: Vacuum cleaner, duster, cleaning cloths.
   c. Hand Tools: For assembling or adjusting storage solutions.
   Examples: Screwdrivers, hammer, pliers.
3. **Technology Tools**
   a. Computer and Software: For managing business operations and creating plans.
   Examples:
   - Microsoft Office or Google Workspace: For documentation and spreadsheets.
   - Trello or Asana: For project management.
   - Evernote or Notion: For notes and organization.
   b. Design and Planning Software: For creating layout plans and visualizing organizational solutions.
   Examples:
   - SketchUp: For 3D modeling.
   - Roomstyler: For room design and layout.
   - Homestyler: For interior design and space planning.
   c. Digital Camera or Smartphone: For documenting before-and-after photos and creating portfolios.
   Examples: High-quality digital camera, smartphone with a good camera.
4. **Business Management Tools**
   a. Scheduling Software: For managing appointments and consultations.

Examples: Calendly, Acuity Scheduling, SimplyBook.me.
  b. Client Management Software (CRM): For tracking client interactions, preferences, and project details.
  Examples: HubSpot CRM, Zoho CRM, Salesforce.
  c. Invoicing and Accounting Software: For managing finances and generating invoices.
  Examples: QuickBooks, FreshBooks, Xero.
  d. Project Management Tools: For planning and tracking organizing projects.
  Examples: Asana, Trello, Monday.com.

5. **Marketing and Branding Tools**
  a. Website Builder: For creating a professional online presence.
  Examples: WordPress, Wix, Squarespace.
  b. Social Media Management Tools: For managing social media profiles and scheduling posts.
  Examples: Hootsuite, Buffer, Later.
  c. Graphic Design Software: For creating marketing materials and branding.
  Examples: Canva, Adobe Photoshop, Adobe Illustrator.
  d. Business Cards and Marketing Materials: For distributing information about your services.
  Examples: Printed business cards, brochures, flyers.

6. **Client Communication Tools**
   a. Email Management: For professional communication with clients.
      Examples: Gmail, Outlook, Mailchimp (for newsletters).
   b. Video Conferencing Tools: For virtual consultations and meetings.
      Examples: Zoom, Microsoft Teams, Google Meet.
   c. Proposal and Contract Templates: For formalizing agreements with clients.
      Examples: Microsoft Word or Google Docs templates, contract management software.

7. **Legal and Compliance Tools**
   a. Licensing and Permits: Ensure compliance with local regulations and obtain necessary licenses.
      Examples: Business license, any specific permits required for organizing services.

8. **Professional Development**
   a. Training and Certification: For enhancing skills and credentials.
      Examples: Certifications from organizing associations or courses on professional organizing.
   b. Industry Research: For staying updated on trends and best practices.
      Examples: Industry magazines, online forums, organizing blogs.

By equipping yourself with these tools and resources, you'll be well-prepared to start and run a successful professional organizing business. Focus on providing high-quality, efficient organizing solutions, maintaining a professional appearance, and effectively marketing your services to attract and retain clients.

32. Event Photography

Event photography services capture special moments and memories at weddings, parties, and corporate events. Entrepreneurs with photography skills and equipment can offer coverage packages, photo editing, and album design services, preserving clients' cherished memories.

Starting an event photography business involves capturing high-quality images at various events such as weddings, parties, corporate functions, and more. To do this effectively, you'll need a combination of high-quality photographic equipment, business tools, and client management resources. Here's a comprehensive list of the essential tools and resources you'll need:

1. Photography Equipment
   a. Cameras: High-quality cameras are crucial for capturing sharp, detailed images.
      Examples:
      - DSLR Cameras: Canon EOS 5D Mark IV, Nikon D850.
      - Mirrorless Cameras: Sony Alpha a7 III, Canon EOS R5.
   b. Lenses: Different lenses are used for various types of shots.
      Examples:
      - Standard Zoom Lens: 24-70mm f/2.8.
      - Wide-Angle Lens: 16-35mm f/2.8.
      - Prime Lens: 50mm f/1.8 or 85mm f/1.4 for portraits.

c. Tripods and Monopods: For stable shots and long exposures.
   Examples: Manfrotto Tripod, Joby GorillaPod, monopods for mobility.
d. Lighting Equipment: For controlling and enhancing lighting conditions.
   Examples:
   - External Flash Units: Speedlite (Canon), SB-700 (Nikon).
   - Softboxes and Umbrellas: For diffusing light.
   - Continuous Lighting: LED panels for constant light.
e. Memory Cards and Storage: For storing and managing digital photos.
   Examples: High-capacity SD cards (64GB or higher), external hard drives, cloud storage solutions (e.g., Dropbox, Google Drive).
f. Camera Bag: For carrying and protecting your equipment.
   Examples: Lowepro ProTactic, Think Tank Photo Airport Essentials.
g. Camera Accessories: Additional tools to enhance your shooting experience.
   Examples: Lens cleaning kit, extra batteries, battery charger, remote shutter release.

2. Editing and Post-Production Tools
a. Computer: A powerful computer for processing and editing photos.
   Examples: Apple MacBook Pro, high-performance Windows PC.

b. Editing Software: For photo editing and retouching.
   Examples:
   - Adobe Lightroom: For managing and editing photos.
   - Adobe Photoshop: For advanced editing and retouching.
   - Capture One: Professional photo editing and color grading.
c. Calibration Tools: For ensuring color accuracy on your monitor.
   Examples: Color calibration tool like X-Rite i1Display Pro.

3. Business Management Tools

a. Scheduling and Booking Software: For managing appointments and event bookings.
   Examples: Calendly, Acuity Scheduling, SimplyBook.me.
b. Client Management Software (CRM): For tracking client interactions and managing details.
   Examples:* HubSpot CRM, Zoho CRM, Salesforce.
c. Invoicing and Accounting Software: For managing finances and generating invoices.
   Examples: QuickBooks, FreshBooks, Xero.
d. Contract and Proposal Templates: For formalizing agreements with clients.
   Examples: Microsoft Word or Google Docs templates, contract management software like HelloSign.

4. **Marketing and Branding Tools**
   a. Website Builder: For creating a professional portfolio and online presence.
      <u>Examples:</u> WordPress, Wix, Squarespace.
   b. Portfolio Hosting: For showcasing your work to potential clients.
      <u>Examples:</u> SmugMug, Zenfolio, your own website.
   c. Social Media Management Tools: For managing and scheduling social media posts.
      <u>Examples:</u> Hootsuite, Buffer, Later.
   d. Graphic Design Software: For creating marketing materials and branding.
      <u>Examples:</u> Canva, Adobe Photoshop, Adobe Illustrator.
   e. Business Cards and Marketing Materials: For distributing information about your services.
      <u>Examples:</u> Printed business cards, brochures, flyers.

5. **Client Communication Tools**
   a. Email Management: For professional communication with clients.
      <u>Examples:</u> Gmail, Outlook, Mailchimp (for newsletters).
   b. Video Conferencing Tools: For virtual consultations and meetings.
      <u>Examples:</u> Zoom, Microsoft Teams, Google Meet.

6. Legal and Compliance Tools
   a. Model Release Forms: To obtain permission from clients or subjects to use their images.
   <u>Examples:</u> Standard model release form templates.

7. Workspace Setup
   a. Photo Editing Workspace: For editing and processing photos.
   <u>Examples</u>: Dual monitors, comfortable desk setup, printer for proofs.

8. Professional Development
   a. Training and Workshops: For improving photography skills and staying updated with industry trends.
   <u>Examples</u>: Online courses, photography workshops, industry conferences.
   b. Networking: For connecting with other professionals and potential clients.
   <u>Examples</u>: Photography associations, local business groups, social media groups.

By equipping yourself with these tools and resources, you'll be well-prepared to start and run a successful event photography business. Focus on delivering high-quality images, maintaining a professional appearance, and effectively marketing your services to attract and retain clients.

33. Portrait Photography

Portrait photography services cater to individuals and families looking to capture their milestones and personalities in timeless images. Entrepreneurs can offer studio or outdoor sessions, customized packages, and fine art prints, creating lasting keepsakes for their clients.

Starting a portrait photography business involves capturing high-quality images of individuals or groups, often in a studio or specific settings. To ensure you can provide exceptional service and manage your business effectively, you'll need a combination of photographic equipment, editing tools, and business management resources. Here's a comprehensive list of the essential tools and resources you'll need:

1. Photography Equipment
- a. Cameras: High-quality cameras are crucial for capturing detailed portraits.
  Examples:
    - DSLR Cameras: Canon EOS 5D Mark IV, Nikon D850.
    - Mirrorless Cameras: Sony Alpha a7 III, Canon EOS R5.
- b. Lenses: Different lenses provide various perspectives and effects.
  Examples:
    - Portrait Lens: 85mm f/1.4 or 50mm f/1.8 for sharp, flattering portraits.
    - Standard Zoom Lens: 24-70mm f/2.8 for versatility in framing.

c. Lighting Equipment: Essential for controlling lighting conditions and creating the desired mood.
   Examples:
   - External Flash Units: Canon Speedlite, Nikon SB-700.
   - Softboxes and Umbrellas: For diffusing light and reducing harsh shadows.
   - Continuous Lighting: LED panels for consistent lighting.
d. Backdrops: For creating a clean and controlled background.
   Examples: Various colored or textured backdrops, collapsible or retractable background systems.
e. Tripods and Light Stands: For stability and positioning lighting and camera equipment.
   Examples: Manfrotto Tripod, Neewer Light Stands.
f. Reflectors and Diffusers: For modifying and controlling light.
   Examples: 5-in-1 reflectors, diffusing panels.

g. Camera Bag: For transporting and protecting your equipment.
   Examples: Lowepro ProTactic, Think Tank Photo Airport Essentials.
h. Memory Cards and Storage: For storing high-resolution images.

Examples: High-capacity SD cards (64GB or higher), external hard drives, cloud storage solutions (e.g., Dropbox, Google Drive).
  i. Cleaning Supplies: For maintaining your camera and lenses.
     Examples: Lens cleaning kit, microfiber cloths, air blower.

2. **Editing and Post-Production Tools**
   a. Computer: A powerful computer for processing and editing photos.
      Examples: Apple MacBook Pro, high-performance Windows PC.
   b. Editing Software: For retouching and enhancing portraits.
      Examples:
      - Adobe Lightroom: For managing and editing photos.
      - Adobe Photoshop: For advanced editing and retouching.
      - Capture One: For professional photo editing and color grading.
   c. Calibration Tools: For ensuring accurate color representation on your monitor.
      Examples: X-Rite i1Display Pro.

3. **Business Management Tools**
   a. Scheduling and Booking Software: For managing client appointments and photo sessions.
      Examples: Calendly, Acuity Scheduling, SimplyBook.me.

b. Client Management Software (CRM): For tracking client interactions and managing details.
   Examples: HubSpot CRM, Zoho CRM, Salesforce.
c. Invoicing and Accounting Software: For managing finances and generating invoices.
   Examples: QuickBooks, FreshBooks, Xero.
d. Contract and Proposal Templates: For formalizing agreements with clients.
   Examples: Microsoft Word or Google Docs templates, contract management software like HelloSign.

4. Marketing and Branding Tools

a. Website Builder: For creating an online portfolio and showcasing your work.
   Examples: WordPress, Wix, Squarespace.
b. Portfolio Hosting: For displaying your best work to potential clients.
   Examples: SmugMug, Zenfolio, your own website.
c. Social Media Management Tools: For managing and scheduling posts on social media platforms.
   Examples: Hootsuite, Buffer, Later.
d. Graphic Design Software: For creating marketing materials and branding.
   Examples: Canva, Adobe Photoshop, Adobe Illustrator.
e. Business Cards and Marketing Materials: For distributing information about your services.

Examples: Printed business cards, brochures, flyers.

5. Client Communication Tools
   a. Email Management: For professional communication with clients.
      Examples: Gmail, Outlook, Mailchimp (for newsletters).
   b. Video Conferencing Tools: For virtual consultations and meetings.
      Examples: Zoom, Microsoft Teams, Google Meet.
   c. Proposal and Contract Templates: For formalizing agreements with clients.
      Examples: Microsoft Word or Google Docs templates, contract management software.

6. Workspace Setup
   a. Studio Equipment: For setting up a dedicated space for studio portraits.
      Examples: Backdrop stands, studio lighting, props.
   b. Office Furniture: For a functional and comfortable workspace.
      Examples: Desk, ergonomic chair, shelving for equipment storage.

7. Professional Development
   a. Training and Workshops: For improving photography skills and staying updated with industry trends.
      Examples: Online courses, photography workshops, industry conferences.

b. Networking: For connecting with other professionals and potential clients.
   <u>Examples</u>: Photography associations, local business groups, social media groups.

By equipping yourself with these tools and resources, you'll be well-prepared to start and run a successful portrait photography business. Focus on delivering high-quality portraits, maintaining a professional appearance, and effectively marketing your services to attract and retain clients.

34. Product Photography

Product photography services help businesses showcase their merchandise in high-quality images for marketing and e-commerce purposes. Entrepreneurs can offer professional lighting, styling, and editing services, helping clients attract customers and increase sales.

Starting a product photography business involves capturing high-quality images of products for marketing, e-commerce, catalogs, and more. To deliver professional results and manage your business efficiently, you'll need a variety of specialized tools and resources. Here's a comprehensive list of the essential tools and equipment you'll need:

1. Photography Equipment
    a. Cameras: High-resolution cameras are essential for capturing detailed product images.
    Examples:
- DSLR Cameras: Canon EOS 5D Mark IV, Nikon D850.
- Mirrorless Cameras: Sony Alpha a7 III, Canon EOS R5.

    b. Lenses: Different lenses are used to capture product details and different angles.
    Examples:
- Macro Lens: For close-up shots of small products (e.g., 100mm f/2.8 macro).

- Standard Zoom Lens: For versatile shooting (e.g., 24-70mm f/2.8).
- Wide-Angle Lens: For larger products or wider scenes (e.g., 16-35mm f/4).

c. Tripods and Light Stands: For stability and precise positioning of the camera and lighting.
   Examples: Manfrotto Tripod, Neewer Light Stands.

d. Lighting Equipment: Essential for achieving consistent and controlled lighting.
   Examples:
   - Softboxes and Umbrellas: To diffuse light and reduce harsh shadows.
   - Continuous Lighting: LED panels or fluorescent lights for consistent illumination.
   - External Flash Units: For additional light sources if needed.

d. Light Tents and Diffusers: For creating a controlled lighting environment and reducing reflections.
   Examples: Light tents, collapsible diffusers, and reflectors.

e. Backdrops: For creating clean, distraction-free backgrounds.
   Examples: Various colors or textures of seamless paper or fabric backdrops.

f. Camera Bag: For carrying and protecting your camera and accessories.

      Examples: Lowepro ProTactic, Think Tank Photo Airport Essentials.
- g. Memory Cards and Storage: For storing high-resolution images.
  Examples: High-capacity SD cards (64GB or higher), external hard drives, cloud storage solutions (e.g., Dropbox, Google Drive).
- h. Cleaning Supplies: For maintaining your camera and lenses.
  Examples: Lens cleaning kit, microfiber cloths, air blower.

2. Editing and Post-Production Tools

- a. Computer: A powerful computer for processing and editing photos.
  Examples: Apple MacBook Pro, high-performance Windows PC.
- b. Editing Software: For photo editing and retouching.
  Examples:
    - Adobe Lightroom: For managing and editing photos.
    - Adobe Photoshop: For advanced editing and retouching.
    - Capture One: Professional photo editing and color grading.
- c. Calibration Tools: For ensuring color accuracy on your monitor.
  Examples: Color calibration tool like X-Rite i1Display Pro.

3. Business Management Tools

a. Scheduling and Booking Software: For managing appointments and event bookings.
   <u>Examples:</u> Calendly, Acuity Scheduling, SimplyBook.me.
b. Client Management Software (CRM): For tracking client interactions and managing details.
   <u>Examples:</u>* HubSpot CRM, Zoho CRM, Salesforce.
c. Invoicing and Accounting Software: For managing finances and generating invoices.
   <u>Examples:</u> QuickBooks, FreshBooks, Xero.
d. Contract and Proposal Templates: For formalizing agreements with clients.
   <u>Examples:</u> Microsoft Word or Google Docs templates, contract management software like HelloSign.

4. Marketing and Branding Tools

a. Website Builder: For creating a professional portfolio and online presence.
   <u>Examples:</u> WordPress, Wix, Squarespace.
b. Portfolio Hosting: For showcasing your work to potential clients.
   <u>Examples:</u> SmugMug, Zenfolio, your own website.
c. Social Media Management Tools: For managing and scheduling social media posts.
   <u>Examples:</u> Hootsuite, Buffer, Later.
d. Graphic Design Software: For creating marketing materials and branding.

Examples: Canva, Adobe Photoshop, Adobe Illustrator.
e. Business Cards and Marketing Materials: For distributing information about your services.
Examples: Printed business cards, brochures, flyers.

5. Client Communication Tools
a. Email Management: For professional communication with clients.
Examples: Gmail, Outlook, Mailchimp (for newsletters).
b. Video Conferencing Tools: For virtual consultations and meetings.
Examples: Zoom, Microsoft Teams, Google Meet.

6. Legal and Compliance Tools
a. Model Release Forms: To obtain permission from clients or subjects to use their product images.
Examples: Standard model release form templates.

7. Workspace Setup
a. Studio Equipment: For setting up a dedicated space for product photography.
Examples: Backdrop stands, product display tables, studio lighting setups.
b. Office Furniture: For a comfortable and functional workspace.
Examples: Desk, ergonomic chair, shelving for equipment storage.

8. Professional Development
   a. Training and Workshops: For improving photography skills and staying updated with industry trends.
      Examples: Online courses, photography workshops, industry conferences.
   b. Networking: For connecting with other professionals and potential clients.
      Examples: Photography associations, local business groups, social media groups.

By equipping yourself with these tools and resources, you'll be well-prepared to start and run a successful product photography business. Focus on delivering high-quality images, maintaining a professional appearance, and effectively marketing your services to attract and retain clients.

35. Real Estate Photography

Real estate photography services highlight properties for sale or rent with stunning visual imagery. Entrepreneurs can offer interior and exterior photography, virtual tours, and aerial drone shots, helping real estate agents and property owners market their listings effectively.

Starting a real estate photography business involves capturing high-quality images of properties for use in listings, marketing materials, and virtual tours. To succeed in this field, you'll need a combination of specialized photography equipment, editing tools, and business management resources. Here's a comprehensive list of the essential tools and equipment you'll need:

1. Photography Equipment
    a. Cameras: High-resolution cameras are crucial for capturing detailed property images.

Examples:
- DSLR Cameras: Canon EOS 5D Mark IV, Nikon D850.
- Mirrorless Cameras: Sony Alpha a7 III, Canon EOS R5.

    b. Lenses: Wide-angle lenses are essential for capturing the full scope of rooms and spaces.

Examples
- Wide-Angle Lens: 16-35mm f/4 or 14-24mm f/2.8 for capturing entire rooms.
- Tilt-Shift Lens: Canon TS-E 24mm f/3.5L or Nikon PC-E 24mm f/3.5D for

correcting distortion and capturing straight lines.

c. Tripods: For stable shots and precise positioning.
   <u>Examples</u> Manfrotto 190XPRO, Gitzo GT1545T.
d. Lighting Equipment: Useful for interior shots, especially in poorly lit areas.
   <u>Examples:</u>
   - External Flash Units: Canon Speedlite 600EX II-RT, Nikon SB-5000.
   - Continuous Lighting: LED panels for consistent illumination.
e. Reflectors and Diffusers: For controlling and modifying light. If not using then need a very sunny day with all the lights on in each room.
   <u>Examples</u>: 5-in-1 reflectors, diffusing panels.
f. Camera Accessories: To support various aspects of shooting and editing.
   <u>Examples</u> Remote shutter release, spare batteries, memory cards (high-capacity SD cards), lens cleaning kit.
g. Drones: For aerial shots and capturing the property from unique angles.
   <u>Examples</u>: DJI Mavic Air 2, DJI Phantom 4 Pro.

2. Editing and Post-Production Tools
   a. Computer: A powerful computer for processing and editing photos.

Examples Apple MacBook Pro, high-performance Windows PC.
  b. Editing Software: For retouching and enhancing property images.
  Examples
  - Adobe Lightroom: For organizing and basic editing.
  - Adobe Photoshop: For advanced editing and retouching.
  - Photomatix Pro or Aurora HDR: For creating HDR images of interiors.
  c. Calibration Tools: For ensuring color accuracy on your monitor.
  Examples: X-Rite i1Display Pro.

3. **Business Management Tools**
   a. Scheduling and Booking Software. For managing client appointments and photo shoots.
   Examples; Calendly, Acuity Scheduling, SimplyBook.me.
   b. Client Management Software (CRM): For tracking client interactions and managing details.
   Examples: HubSpot CRM, Zoho CRM, Salesforce.
   c. Invoicing and Accounting Software: For managing finances and generating invoices.
   Examples: QuickBooks, FreshBooks, Xero.
   d. Contract and Proposal Templates: For formalizing agreements with clients.

Examples Microsoft Word or Google Docs templates, contract management software like HelloSign.

4. Marketing and Branding Tools
   a. Website Builder: For creating an online portfolio and showcasing your work.
      Examples: WordPress, Wix, Squarespace.
   b. Portfolio Hosting: For displaying your best work to potential clients.
      Examples: SmugMug, Zenfolio, your own website.
   c. Social Media Management Tools: For managing and scheduling posts on social media platforms.
      Examples: Hootsuite, Buffer, Later.
   d. Graphic Design Software: For creating marketing materials and branding.
      Examples: Canva, Adobe Photoshop, Adobe Illustrator.
   e. Business Cards and Marketing Materials: For distributing information about your services.
      Examples: Printed business cards, brochures, flyers.

5. Client Communication Tools
   a. Email Management: For professional communication with clients.
      Examples: Gmail, Outlook, Mailchimp (for newsletters).
   b. Video Conferencing Tools: For virtual consultations and meetings.

Examples: Zoom, Microsoft Teams, Google Meet.

6. Legal and Compliance Tools
a. Property Release Forms: To obtain permission to use images of the property.
Examples: Standard property release form templates.

7. Workspace Setup
a. Studio Equipment: For setting up a dedicated space for interior shots.
Examples: Backdrop stands, product display tables, studio lighting setups.
b. Office Furniture: For a comfortable and functional workspace.
Examples: Desk, ergonomic chair, shelving for equipment storage.

8. Professional Development
a. Training and Workshops: For improving photography skills and staying updated with industry trends.
Examples: Online courses, photography workshops, industry conferences.
b. Networking: For connecting with real estate agents, property managers, and potential clients.
Examples: Real estate associations, local business groups, social media groups.

By equipping yourself with these tools and resources, you'll be well-prepared to start and run a successful real estate photography business. Focus on delivering high-quality images that highlight the best features of properties, maintaining a professional appearance, and effectively marketing your services to attract and retain clients.

36. Videography Services

Videography services cater to businesses and individuals looking to create compelling visual content for marketing and storytelling purposes. Entrepreneurs with video production skills can offer filming, editing, and animation services, helping clients engage their audiences and achieve their goals.

Starting a videography business requires a range of tools and equipment to capture, edit, and deliver high-quality video content. Whether you're focusing on events, corporate videos, or creative projects, you'll need a combination of cameras, audio gear, lighting, editing software, and business management tools. Here's a comprehensive list of essential tools and resources you'll need:

1. Video Equipment
    a. Cameras: High-quality cameras are crucial for capturing clear and professional video.
       Examples:
       - DSLR Cameras: Canon EOS 5D Mark IV, Nikon D850.
       - Mirrorless Cameras: Sony Alpha a7S III, Canon EOS R5.
       - Cinema Cameras: Blackmagic URSA Mini Pro, RED Komodo 6K.
    b. Lenses: Different lenses provide various focal lengths and effects.
       Examples:
       - Wide-Angle Lens: For capturing expansive scenes (e.g., 16-35mm f/2.8).

- Standard Zoom Lens: For versatile shooting (e.g., 24-70mm f/2.8).
- Prime Lens: For low light and sharp focus (e.g., 50mm f/1.8).

c. Tripods and Stabilizers: For steady shots and smooth movement.
Examples:
- Tripods: Manfrotto 504X, Benro S6.
- Gimbals/Stabilizers: DJI Ronin-S, Zhiyun Crane 2.

d. Audio Equipment: High-quality audio is crucial for professional video production.
Examples:
- Lavalier Microphones Rode Lavalier GO, Sennheiser EW 112P G4.
- Shotgun Microphones: Rode NTG4+, Sennheiser ME66.
- Audio Recorders: Zoom H5, Tascam DR-60DmkII.

e. Lighting Equipment: For controlling lighting conditions and enhancing video quality.
Examples:
- LED Lights: Aputure Amaran AL-MX, Godox SL-60W.
- Softboxes and Diffusers: For soft, even lighting.
- Ring Lights: For beauty and close-up shots.

f. Backdrops and Props: For creating visually appealing scenes and settings.

Examples: Muslin backdrops, green screens, various props.
   g. Camera Accessories: For additional functionality and convenience.
   Examples: Lens filters, extra batteries, high-capacity memory cards.

2. **Editing and Post-Production Tools**
   a. Computer: A powerful computer for video editing and rendering.
   Examples: Apple MacBook Pro, high-performance Windows PC.
   b. Editing Software: For editing and enhancing video footage.
   Examples:
      - Adobe Premiere Pro: Industry-standard video editing software.
      - Final Cut Pro X: Popular on macOS for professional editing.
      - DaVinci Resolve: Known for its advanced color grading and editing features.
   c. Color Correction Tools: For adjusting and enhancing color in your footage.
   Examples: DaVinci Resolve (built-in), external color grading panels.
   d. Sound Editing Software: For audio post-production.
   Examples: Adobe Audition, Audacity (free).
   e. External Storage: For storing large video files and project backups.

Examples: External hard drives (e.g., Western Digital My Passport), SSDs (e.g., Samsung T7).

3. Business Management Tools
    e. Scheduling and Booking Software. For managing client appointments and photo shoots.
Examples; Calendly, Acuity Scheduling, SimplyBook.me.
    f. Client Management Software (CRM): For tracking client interactions and managing details.
Examples: HubSpot CRM, Zoho CRM, Salesforce.
    g. Invoicing and Accounting Software: For managing finances and generating invoices.
Examples: QuickBooks, FreshBooks, Xero.
    h. Contract and Proposal Templates: For formalizing agreements with clients.
Examples Microsoft Word or Google Docs templates, contract management software like HelloSign.

4. Marketing and Branding Tools
    f. Website Builder: For creating an online portfolio and showcasing your work.
Examples: WordPress, Wix, Squarespace.
    g. Portfolio Hosting: For displaying your best work to potential clients.
Examples: SmugMug, Zenfolio, your own website.

- h. Social Media Management Tools: For managing and scheduling posts on social media platforms.
  Examples: Hootsuite, Buffer, Later.
- i. Graphic Design Software: For creating marketing materials and branding.
  Examples: Canva, Adobe Photoshop, Adobe Illustrator.
- j. Business Cards and Marketing Materials: For distributing information about your services.
  Examples: Printed business cards, brochures, flyers.

5. Client Communication Tools

- c. Email Management: For professional communication with clients.
  Examples: Gmail, Outlook, Mailchimp (for newsletters).
- d. Video Conferencing Tools: For virtual consultations and meetings.
  Examples: Zoom, Microsoft Teams, Google Meet.

6. Legal and Compliance Tools

- b. Property Release Forms: To obtain permission to use images of the property.
  Examples: Standard property release form templates.

7. Workspace Setup

- c. Studio Equipment: For setting up a dedicated space for interior shots.
  Examples: Backdrop stands, product display tables, studio lighting setups.

d. Office Furniture: For a comfortable and functional workspace.
   Examples: Desk, ergonomic chair, shelving for equipment storage.

8. Professional Development
   c. Training and Workshops: For improving photography skills and staying updated with industry trends.
   Examples: Online courses, photography workshops, industry conferences.
   d. Networking: For connecting with real estate agents, property managers, and potential clients.
   Examples: Real estate associations, local business groups, social media groups.

By equipping yourself with these tools and resources, you'll be well-prepared to start and run a successful videography business. Focus on delivering high-quality video content, maintaining a professional appearance, and effectively marketing your services to attract and retain clients.

37. Drone Photography

Drone photography services capture aerial perspectives of landscapes, events, and real estate properties. Entrepreneurs with drone piloting skills and equipment can offer high-resolution imagery and video footage, providing unique visual experiences for their clients.

Starting a drone photography business involves a blend of high-quality drone equipment, photographic tools, and business resources. Here's a comprehensive list of the essential tools and equipment you'll need:

launch and run a successful drone photography business:

1. Drone Equipment
   a. Drones: The core equipment for capturing aerial photographs and videos.
   Examples:
   - DJI Mavic Air 2: Compact, with excellent camera quality and intelligent shooting modes.
   - DJI Phantom 4 Pro V2.0: Known for its high-quality camera and longer flight time.
   - DJI Inspire 2: Professional-grade drone with advanced features for high-end production.
   b. Camera Gimbals: Stabilizes the camera to ensure smooth footage.

Examples: Most high-end drones come with built-in gimbals, but additional gimbals can be used for other camera setups if needed.
c. Spare Batteries: Extra batteries ensure extended flight time and less downtime.
Examples: DJI batteries specific to your drone model.
d. Battery Charger: For recharging multiple batteries simultaneously.
Examples: DJI Intelligent Flight Battery Charger.
e. Memory Cards: For storing high-resolution photos and videos.
Examples: SanDisk Extreme Pro 64GB or higher.
f. Propellers: Spare propellers in case of damage or wear.
Examples: Replacement propellers specific to your drone model.
g. Drone Case or Backpack: For transporting and protecting your drone and accessories.
Examples: DJI Care Refresh, Lowepro DroneGuard.
h. ND Filters: Neutral density filters reduce glare and improve video quality.
Examples: DJI ND Filters, PolarPro ND Filters.
i. Drone Landing Pad: Provides a clean surface for takeoff and landing, protecting the drone from debris.

Examples: Neewer 75cm Foldable Landing Pad.

2. Photography and Videography Equipment

a. Cameras: High-quality cameras for ground-based shots or backup.
   Examples: Canon EOS 5D Mark IV, Sony Alpha a7 III.
b. Lenses: Lenses for different photography needs.
   Examples: 24-70mm f/2.8 for versatile shooting, 50mm f/1.8 for low light.
c. Tripods and Stabilizers: For stable ground-based shots.
   Examples: Manfrotto 190XPRO, Zhiyun Crane 2 for stabilizing.
d. Lighting Equipment: For ground-based shoots to complement drone footage.
   Examples: Godox V1, Aputure Amaran.

3. Editing and Post-Production Tools

a. Computer: A powerful computer for processing and editing photos and videos.
   Examples: Apple MacBook Pro, high-performance Windows PC.
b. Editing Software: For editing and enhancing aerial photos and videos.
   Examples:
   - Adobe Lightroom: For photo editing.
   - Adobe Premiere Pro: For video editing.
   - Final Cut Pro X: Popular for video editing on macOS.

- DaVinci Resolve: For color correction and advanced editing.
c. Color Correction Tools: For adjusting color balance and grading.
Examples: DaVinci Resolve (built-in tools), external color grading panels.
d. External Storage: For backing up and storing large video files.
Examples: External hard drives (e.g., Western Digital My Passport), SSDs (e.g., Samsung T7).

4. Business Management Tools
a. Scheduling and Booking Software. For managing client appointments and projects.
Examples; Calendly, Acuity Scheduling, SimplyBook.me.
b. Client Management Software (CRM): For tracking client interactions and managing details.
Examples: HubSpot CRM, Zoho CRM, Salesforce.
c. Invoicing and Accounting Software: For managing finances and generating invoices.
Examples: QuickBooks, FreshBooks, Xero.
d. Contract and Proposal Templates: For formalizing agreements with clients.
Examples Microsoft Word or Google Docs templates, contract management software like HelloSign.

5. Marketing and Branding Tools
   a. Website Builder: For creating an online portfolio and showcasing your work.
      Examples: WordPress, Wix, Squarespace.
   b. Portfolio Hosting: For displaying your best work to potential clients.
      Examples: Vimeo Pro, YouTube channel, your own website.
   c. Social Media Management Tools: For managing and scheduling posts on social media platforms.
      Examples: Hootsuite, Buffer, Later.
   d. Graphic Design Software: For creating marketing materials and branding.
      Examples: Canva, Adobe Photoshop, Adobe Illustrator.
   e. Business Cards and Marketing Materials: For distributing information about your services.
      Examples: Printed business cards, brochures, flyers.

6. Client Communication Tools
   a. Email Management: For professional communication with clients.
      Examples: Gmail, Outlook, Mailchimp (for newsletters).
   b. Video Conferencing Tools: For virtual consultations and meetings.
      Examples: Zoom, Microsoft Teams, Google Meet.

7. **Legal and Compliance Tools**
    a. Business Insurance: To protect against liabilities and damages.
       <u>Examples:</u> General liability insurance, drone insurance.
    b. Licensing and Permits: Ensure compliance with local regulations and obtain necessary licenses.
       <u>Examples:</u> FAA Part 107 Remote Pilot Certification (for the U.S.), local drone operation permits.
    c. Property Release Forms: To obtain permission to use footage of individuals and property.
       <u>Examples:</u> Talent release form or standard release templates.
8. **Workspace Setup**
    a. Studio Equipment: For setting up a dedicated space for video shoots.
       <u>Examples:</u> Backdrop stands, product display tables, studio lighting setups.
    b. Office Furniture: For a comfortable and functional workspace.
       <u>Examples:</u> Desk, ergonomic chair, shelving for equipment storage.
9. **Professional Development**
    a. Training and Workshops: For improving drone piloting, photography skills, and staying updated with industry trends.
       <u>Examples:</u> Online courses, Drone workshops, industry conferences.

b. Networking: For connecting with real estate agents, property managers, and potential clients.
   Examples: Drone associations, local business groups, social media groups.

By equipping yourself with these tools and resources, you'll be well-prepared to start and run a successful drone photography business. Focus on delivering high-quality aerial imagery, maintaining a professional appearance, and effectively marketing your services to attract and retain clients.

38. Digital Illustration

Digital illustration services create custom artwork for books, magazines, websites, and marketing materials. Entrepreneurs with artistic talent and digital design skills can offer illustration commissions, graphic novels, and character designs, catering to diverse creative projects.

Starting a digital illustration business involves creating artwork using digital tools and software. To effectively run your business, you'll need a combination of hardware and software, as well as business management resources. Here's a comprehensive list of essential tools and resources for launching a digital illustration business:

1. Hardware
   a. Computer: A powerful computer is essential for running illustration software and handling large files.
   Examples:
   - Desktop: Apple iMac Pro, Windows PC with high-end specs.
   - Laptop: Apple MacBook Pro, Microsoft Surface Laptop.

   b. Graphics Tablet: A tablet with a stylus is crucial for precise drawing and illustration.
   Examples:
   - Wacom Cintiq: Professional-grade tablets with a built-in screen.
   - Huion Kamvas: Alternative to Wacom, often more budget-friendly.

- Wacom Intuos Pro: Popular for its sensitivity and versatility.
c. Monitor: A high-resolution monitor helps you see details clearly.
<u>Examples:</u> Dell Ultrasharp U2720Q, BenQ PD3200U.
d. Stylus/Pen: Used with graphics tablets for digital drawing.
<u>Examples:</u> Wacom Pro Pen 2, Huion PW500.
e. External Storage: For backing up and storing large illustration files.
<u>Examples:</u> External hard drives (e.g., Western Digital My Passport), SSDs (e.g., Samsung T7).
f. Backup System: To ensure data safety and avoid loss of work.
<u>Examples:</u> Cloud storage services (e.g., Google Drive, Dropbox), RAID systems.

2. Software
a. Illustration Software: Essential for creating and editing digital illustrations.
<u>Examples:</u>
- Adobe Illustrator: Industry-standard vector graphic software.
- Adobe Photoshop: Popular for raster graphics and detailed artwork.
- CorelDRAW: Alternative to Adobe Illustrator with vector graphic capabilities.
- Clip Studio Paint Favored for comic and manga creation.

- Procreate: Popular iPad app for digital painting and sketching.
  b. Color Management Tools: For accurate color representation and consistency.
  <u>Examples:</u> Adobe Color, Pantone Color Manager.
  c. File Management Software: For organizing and managing your digital files.
  <u>Examples:</u> Adobe Bridge, ACDSee Photo Studio.

4. Business Management Tools
   a. Scheduling and Booking Software. For managing client appointments and project deadlines.
   <u>Examples</u>; Calendly, Acuity Scheduling, SimplyBook.me.
   b. Client Management Software (CRM): For tracking client interactions and managing details.
   <u>Examples</u>: HubSpot CRM, Zoho CRM, Salesforce.
   c. Invoicing and Accounting Software: For managing finances and generating invoices.
   <u>Examples:</u> QuickBooks, FreshBooks, Xero.
   d. Contract and Proposal Templates: For formalizing agreements with clients.
   <u>Examples</u> Microsoft Word or Google Docs templates, contract management software like HelloSign.

4. **Marketing and Branding Tools**
    a. Website Builder: For creating an online portfolio and showcasing your work.
       Examples: WordPress, Wix, Squarespace.
    b. Portfolio Hosting: For displaying your best work to potential clients.
       Examples: Vimeo Pro, YouTube channel, your own website.
    c. Social Media Management Tools: For managing and scheduling posts on social media platforms.
       Examples: Hootsuite, Buffer, Later.
    d. Graphic Design Software: For creating marketing materials and branding.
       Examples: Canva, Adobe Photoshop, Adobe Illustrator.
    e. Business Cards and Marketing Materials: For distributing information about your services.
       Examples: Printed business cards, brochures, flyers.
5. **Client Communication Tools**
    a. Email Management: For professional communication with clients.
       Examples: Gmail, Outlook, Mailchimp (for newsletters).
    b. Video Conferencing Tools: For virtual consultations and meetings.
       Examples: Zoom, Microsoft Teams, Google Meet.

6. Legal and Compliance Tools
   a. Business Insurance: To protect against liabilities and damages.
      <u>Examples:</u> General liability insurance, drone insurance.
   b. Copyright and Usage Agreements: To protect your intellectual property and set terms for usage..
      <u>Examples:</u> Standard copyright agreements, usage rights agreements..

7. Workspace Setup
   a. Work space For setting up a comfortable and efficient workb.space.
      <u>Examples::</u> Adjustable desk, ergonomic chair, good lighting.
   b. Office Furniture: For a functional and organized workspace.
      <u>Examples:</u> Desk with ample workspace, shelving for art supplies and reference materials.

8. Professional Development
   c. Training and Workshops: For improving illustration skills, and staying updated with industry trends.
      <u>Examples:</u> Online courses, Illustration workshops, industry conferences.
   d. Networking: For connecting with artists and potential clients.
      <u>Examples:</u> Art associations, online forums, social media groups

By investing in these tools and resources, you'll be well-equipped to start and run a successful digital illustration business. Focus on developing your unique style, maintaining high standards of work, and effectively marketing your services to attract and retain clients.

39. Graphic Design

Start here Graphic design services help businesses and individuals communicate visually through logos, branding, and promotional materials. Entrepreneurs with design expertise can offer logo creation, print and digital design, and brand identity packages, helping clients stand out in competitive markets.

Starting a graphic design business requires a combination of hardware, software, and business management tools to create professional designs and run your business efficiently. Here's a comprehensive list of essential tools and resources to help you launch and manage a successful graphic design business:

1. Hardware
- a. Computer: A powerful computer is crucial for running graphic design software and handling large files.
  Examples:
  - Desktop: Apple iMac Pro, high-performance Windows PC.
  - Laptop: Apple MacBook Pro, Microsoft Surface Laptop.
- b. Monitor: A high-resolution monitor helps you see details clearly and ensure accurate color representation.
  Examples: Dell Ultrasharp U2720Q, BenQ PD3200U.
- c. Graphics Tablet: Useful for digital drawing, sketching, and photo editing.

Examples:
- Wacom Cintiq: Professional-grade tablets with a built-in screen.
- Huion Kamvas: Budget-friendly alternative.
- Wacom Intuos Pro: For more detailed drawing and editing.

d. Stylus/Pen: Used with graphics tablets for precise drawing.
   Examples: Wacom Pro Pen 2, Huion PW500.
e. External Storage: For backing up and storing large design files.
   Examples: External hard drives (e.g., Western Digital My Passport), SSDs (e.g., Samsung T7).
f. Backup System: To ensure data safety and avoid loss of work.
   Examples: Cloud storage services (e.g., Google Drive, Dropbox), RAID systems.
g. Printer: For printing design proofs or client materials.
   Examples: Epson SureColor P400, Canon image PROGRAF PRO-1000.

2. Software
a. Graphic Design Software: Essential for creating and editing graphics.
   Examples: -
   - Adobe Creative Cloud: Includes Adobe Illustrator, Photoshop, InDesign, and more.

- CorelDRAW: Alternative vector graphic software.
- Affinity Designer: Budget-friendly vector graphic software.
- Affinity Photo: Alternative to Adobe Photoshop.

b. Vector Graphics Software: For creating and editing vector-based designs.
Examples: Adobe Illustrator, CorelDRAW.

c. Raster Graphics Software: For photo editing and bitmap graphics.
Examples: Adobe Photoshop, Affinity Photo.

d. Layout and Desktop Publishing Software: For creating print and digital layouts.
Examples Adobe InDesign, Affinity Publisher.

e. Color Management Tools: For accurate color representation.
Examples Adobe Color, Pantone Color Manager.

f. File Management Software: For organizing and managing your design files.
Examples: Adobe Bridge, ACDSee Photo Studio.

3. **Business Management Tools**
   a. Scheduling and Booking Software: For managing client appointments and project deadlines.
   Examples Calendly, Acuity Scheduling, SimplyBook.me.

b. **Client Management Software (CRM):** For tracking client interactions and managing details.
   <u>Examples</u> HubSpot CRM, Zoho CRM, Salesforce.
c. **Invoicing and Accounting Software:** For managing finances and generating invoices.
   <u>Examples:</u> QuickBooks, FreshBooks, Xero.
d. **Contract and Proposal Templates:** For formalizing agreements with clients.
   <u>Examples:</u> Microsoft Word or Google Docs templates, contract management software like HelloSign.

4. Marketing and Branding Tools

a. **Website Builder:** For creating an online portfolio and showcasing your work.
   <u>Examples:</u> WordPress, Wix, Squarespace.
c. **Portfolio Hosting:** For displaying your best work to potential clients.
   <u>Examples:</u> Behance, Dribbble, your own website.

c. **Social Media Management Tools:** For managing and scheduling social media posts to promote your work.
   <u>Examples:</u> Hootsuite, Buffer, Later.
d. **Graphic Design Software for Marketing Materials:** For creating business cards, brochures, and other marketing materials.
   <u>Examples</u> Canva, Adobe Illustrator, Adobe Photoshop.

e. **Business Cards and Marketing Materials:** For distributing information about your services.
      <u>Examples:</u> Printed business cards, brochures, flyers.

5. Client Communication Tools
   a. **Email Management:** For professional communication with clients.
      <u>Examples:</u> Gmail, Outlook, Mailchimp (for newsletters).
   b. **Video Conferencing Tools:** For virtual consultations and meetings with clients.
      <u>Examples:</u> Zoom, Microsoft Teams, Google Meet.

6. Legal and Compliance Tools
   a. **Business Insurance:** To protect against liabilities and damages.
      <u>Examples:</u> General liability insurance, professional liability insurance.
   b. **Licensing and Permits:** Ensure compliance with local regulations and obtain necessary licenses.
      <u>Examples:</u> Business license, any specific permits required for operating your business.
   c. **Copyright and Usage Agreements:** To protect your intellectual property and set terms for usage.
      <u>Examples:</u> Standard copyright agreements, usage rights agreements.

7. Workspace Setup
   a. **Studio Equipment:** For setting up a comfortable and efficient workspace.

      Examples: Adjustable desk, ergonomic chair, good lighting.
  b. Office Furniture: For a functional and organized workspace.
      Examples: Desk with ample workspace, shelving for art supplies and reference materials.

8. Professional Development

  a. Training and Workshops: For improving your design skills and staying updated with industry trends.
      Examples: Online courses, graphic design workshops, industry conferences.
  b. Networking: For connecting with other designers and potential clients.
      Examples: Design communities, online forums, social media groups.

By equipping yourself with these tools and resources, you'll be well-prepared to start and run a successful graphic design business. Focus on developing a strong portfolio, maintaining high standards of work, and effectively marketing your services to attract and retain clients.

40. Web Design

Web design services create functional and visually appealing websites for businesses, organizations, and individuals. Entrepreneurs with coding and design skills can offer custom website development, e-commerce solutions, and responsive design optimization, helping clients achieve their online goals.

Starting a web design business requires a combination of technical tools, creative software, and business resources. Here's a comprehensive list of essential tools and equipment you'll need to launch and run a successful web design business:

1. Hardware
  a. Computer: A powerful computer is crucial for running design and development software efficiently.
  Examples:
   - Desktop: Apple iMac Pro, high-performance Windows PC.
   - Laptop: Apple MacBook Pro, Microsoft Surface Laptop.
  b. Monitor: A high-resolution monitor helps with accurate design and development work.
  Examples: Dell Ultrasharp U2720Q, BenQ PD3200U.
  c. External Storage: For backing up and storing website files, assets, and client data.
  Examples: External hard drives (e.g., Western Digital My Passport), SSDs (e.g., Samsung T7).

    d. **Backup System:** To ensure data safety and avoid loss of work.
   <u>Examples:</u> Cloud storage services (e.g., Google Drive, Dropbox), RAID systems.
    e. **Graphics Tablet (Optional):** Useful for web design tasks involving custom illustrations or detailed graphics.
   <u>Examples:</u> Wacom Cintiq, Huion Kamvas.

2. **Design and Development Software**

   a. **Web Design Software:** Essential for creating and editing website designs.
   <u>Examples:</u>
   - Adobe XD: For UI/UX design and prototyping.
   - Sketch: Popular for web and mobile UI design (Mac only).
   - Figma: Collaborative design tool for UI/UX design.

   b. **Graphic Design Software:** For creating visual elements and assets.
   <u>Examples:</u>
   - Adobe Photoshop: For image editing and graphics.
   - Adobe Illustrator: For vector graphics and illustrations.
   - Affinity Designer: Alternative to Adobe Illustrator.

c. Code Editors/IDE: For writing and editing code.
   Examples:
   - Visual Studio Code: Popular code editor with extensions for various programming languages.
   - Sublime Text: Lightweight and powerful code editor.
   - Atom: Open-source code editor with collaboration features.
d. Web Development Frameworks and Libraries: For speeding up development and creating responsive designs.
   Examples:
   - Bootstrap: Popular front-end framework for responsive web design.
   - Foundation: Another responsive front-end framework.
   - Tailwind CSS: Utility-first CSS framework.
e. Content Management Systems (CMS): For managing and building websites.
   Examples:
   - WordPress: Most widely used CMS for various types of websites.
   - Joomla: Flexible CMS for building complex websites.
   - Drupal: Robust CMS for more complex, enterprise-level sites.

f. Browser Testing Tools: For testing websites across different browsers and devices.
   Examples:
   - BrowserStack: Testing tool for cross-browser and cross-device testing.
   - Sauce Labs: Provides cross-browser testing and mobile testing.

3. Business Management Tools

a. Scheduling and Booking Software: For managing client appointments and project deadlines.
   Examples: Calendly, Acuity Scheduling, SimplyBook.me.

b. Client Management Software (CRM): For tracking client interactions and managing details.
   Examples: HubSpot CRM, Zoho CRM, Salesforce.

c. Invoicing and Accounting Software: For managing finances and generating invoices.
   Examples: QuickBooks, FreshBooks, Xero.

d. Project Management Software: For managing projects, tasks, and team collaboration.
   Examples: Asana, Trello, Monday.com.

e. Contract and Proposal Templates: For formalizing agreements with clients.
   Examples: Microsoft Word or Google Docs templates, contract management software like HelloSign.

4. Marketing and Branding Tools
   a. Website Builder: For creating and showcasing your own portfolio website.
      <u>Examples:</u> WordPress, Wix, Squarespace.
   b. Portfolio Hosting: For displaying your best work to potential clients.
      <u>Examples:</u> Behance, Dribbble, your own website.
   c. Social Media Management Tools: For managing and scheduling social media posts to promote your business.
      <u>Examples:</u> Hootsuite, Buffer, Later.
   d. Graphic Design Software for Marketing Materials: For creating business cards, brochures, and other marketing materials.
      <u>Examples:</u> Canva, Adobe Illustrator, Adobe Photoshop.
   e. Business Cards and Marketing Materials: For distributing information about your services.
      <u>Examples:</u> Printed business cards, brochures, flyers.

5. Client Communication Tools
   a. Email Management: For professional communication with clients.
      <u>Examples:</u> Gmail, Outlook, Mailchimp (for newsletters).
   b. Video Conferencing Tools: For virtual consultations and meetings with clients.
      <u>Examples:</u> Zoom, Microsoft Teams, Google Meet.

c. Messaging and Collaboration Tools: For team communication and collaboration.
      <u>Examples:</u> Slack, Microsoft Teams, Discord.

6. Legal and Compliance Tools
   a. Business Insurance: To protect against liabilities and damages.
      <u>Examples:</u> General liability insurance, professional liability insurance.
   b. Licensing and Permits: Ensure compliance with local regulations and obtain necessary licenses.
      <u>Examples:</u> Business license, any specific permits required for operating your business.
   c. Copyright and Usage Agreements: To protect your intellectual property and set terms for usage.
      <u>Examples:</u> Standard copyright agreements, usage rights agreements.

7. Workspace Setup
   a. Studio Equipment: For setting up a comfortable and efficient workspace.
      <u>Examples:</u> Adjustable desk, ergonomic chair, good lighting.
   b. Office Furniture: For a functional and organized workspace.
      <u>Examples:</u> Desk with ample workspace, shelving for equipment and reference materials.

8. Professional Development

   a. **Training and Workshops:** For improving your skills and staying updated with industry trends.
   <u>Examples:</u> Online courses, web design workshops, industry conferences.
   b. **Networking:** For connecting with other professionals and potential clients.
   <u>Examples:</u> Design communities, online forums, social media groups.

By equipping yourself with these tools and resources, you'll be well-prepared to start and run a successful web design business. Focus on delivering high-quality designs, maintaining a professional image, and effectively marketing your services to attract and retain clients.

41. Social Media Management

Social media management services help businesses build and engage their online communities across various platforms. Entrepreneurs with digital marketing skills can offer content creation, scheduling, and analytics reporting services, helping clients enhance their social media presence and drive results.

Skills & Tools: Master social media platforms (Instagram, Facebook, LinkedIn, etc.), content creation, and analytics. Use tools like Canva for graphics, Hootsuite or Buffer for scheduling, and social media analytics tools to track performance.

Portfolio & Online Presence: Build a portfolio showcasing sample social media campaigns or content. Create a professional website or social media pages to highlight your services, client testimonials, and case studies.

Target Audience & Pricing Model: Identify your niche (e.g., small businesses, influencers, etc.) and set competitive pricing packages based on the services offered, such as content creation, social media monitoring, and strategy planning.

42. Content Writing

If with the right tools for writing, editing, managing projects, and communicating with clients. Here's a comprehensive list of tools and resources you'll need to launch and run a successful content writing business:

Starting a content writing business allows you to use your writing skills to create engaging, valuable content for businesses, websites, and publications. With the rise of digital marketing and online presence, businesses need quality content to connect with their audience and improve SEO. By offering services such as blog posts, articles, website copy, and marketing content, you can help clients enhance their brand while building a profitable business.

To succeed in this business, you'll need the right tools for writing, editing, managing projects, and communicating with clients. Here's a comprehensive list of tools and resources you'll need to launch and run a successful content writing business:

1. **Writing & Editing Tools**: You'll need software like Microsoft Word, Google Docs, or Grammarly to write and edit content. These tools help ensure your writing is clear, concise, and error-free.
2. **Project Management Tools**: Platforms like Trello or Asana are essential for managing client projects, deadlines, and collaboration.

They help you stay organized and ensure timely delivery of content.
3. **Client Communication Tools**: Maintaining clear communication with clients is crucial. Use email, Slack, or video conferencing tools like Zoom to discuss project details, feedback, and revisions.

3 Key Things to Start Your Business:
1. **Niche & Specialization**: Decide whether you'll specialize in a specific industry (e.g., tech, finance) or offer general content writing services. Having a niche can set you apart from competitors.
2. **Portfolio & Samples**: Build a portfolio showcasing your writing skills. If you're just starting out, create sample articles or offer free work for initial clients to demonstrate your expertise.
3. **Pricing Structure**: Determine your pricing model—whether you'll charge per word, per project, or on a retainer basis. Competitive, clear pricing is key to attracting clients.

By utilizing these tools and resources, you'll be well-equipped to start and manage a successful content writing business. Focus on delivering high-quality content, maintaining strong client relationships, and staying current with industry trends to build and sustain your business.

43. Copyediting and Proofreading

Copyediting and proofreading services help authors, businesses, and publishers polish their written content for accuracy and clarity. Entrepreneurs with strong language skills and attention to detail can offer editing, proofreading, and manuscript evaluation services, ensuring error-free publications.

Starting a copyediting and proofreading business involves having a set of specialized tools and resources to ensure that your editing work is accurate, efficient, and professional. Here's a detailed list of essential tools and equipment you'll need to launch and run a successful copyediting and proofreading business:

1. Hardware
   a. Computer: A reliable computer is essential for running editing software and managing client files.
      Examples:
- Desktop: High-performance Windows PC or Apple iMac.
- Laptop: Apple MacBook Pro, Microsoft Surface Laptop.

   b. Monitor: A high-resolution monitor helps in viewing and editing documents with clarity.
      Examples: Dell Ultrasharp U2720Q, BenQ PD3200U.

   c. External Storage: For backing up documents, client files, and projects.

Examples: External hard drives (e.g., Western Digital My Passport), SSDs (e.g., Samsung T7).

d. Backup System: To ensure data safety and prevent loss of work.
Examples: Cloud storage services (e.g., Google Drive, Dropbox), RAID systems.

2. **Editing and Proofreading Tools**
   a. Word Processing Software: Essential for drafting and editing documents.
   Examples:
      - -Microsoft Word: Industry-standard word processing software with editing and tracking features.
      - Google Docs: Cloud-based tool for drafting, editing, and collaborating.
   b. Grammar and Style Checkers: Tools for improving grammar, style, and readability.
   Examples:
      - Grammarly: Checks grammar, punctuation, style, and offers suggestions.
      - ProWritingAid: Comprehensive tool for grammar checking, style improvements, and writing analysis.
      - Hemingway Editor: Enhances readability and sentence structure.
   c. Plagiarism Checkers: To ensure content originality and detect unintentional plagiarism.

Examples:
- Copyscape: Detects duplicate content and plagiarism.
- Turnitin: Used for thorough plagiarism detection and originality checking.

d. Reference and Style Guides: For adhering to specific formatting and style guidelines.
Examples:
- The Chicago Manual of Style: Comprehensive guide for style and citation.
- The Associated Press (AP) Stylebook: Commonly used for journalistic and business writing.
- APA Style Manual: For academic and research writing.

3. Project Management and Client Communication Tools

a. Project Management Software: For managing editing projects, deadlines, and client communications.
Examples:
- Asana: Task and project management with timeline and task tracking.
- Trello: Visual project management tool using boards and lists.
- Monday.com: Comprehensive project management and team collaboration tool.

b. **Client Management Software (CRM):** For managing client information, interactions, and maintaining records.
   Examples:
   - HubSpot CRM: Manages client relationships and tracks interactions.
   - Zoho CRM: Comprehensive CRM tool for client management.

c. **Invoicing and Accounting Software:** For managing invoices, tracking payments, and handling finances.
   Examples:
   - QuickBooks: Comprehensive accounting software with invoicing capabilities.
   - FreshBooks: User-friendly tool for invoicing and accounting.
   - Xero: Online accounting software with invoicing features.

d. **Contract and Proposal Templates:** For formalizing agreements with clients and outlining project scopes.
   Examples:
   - HelloSign: Electronic signature and document management tool.
   - PandaDoc: For creating, sending, and managing contracts and proposals.

4. **Marketing and Branding Tools**
   a. **Website Builder:** For creating a professional website to showcase your services and portfolio.

Examples:
- WordPress: Popular website builder with various customization options.
- Wix: Easy-to-use website builder with design templates.
- Squarespace: Website builder with a focus on design and aesthetics.

b. Portfolio Hosting: For displaying samples of your editing and proofreading work.

Examples:
- Behance: Platform for showcasing creative work.
- Dribbble: Community for creatives to display their portfolios.

c. Social Media Management: For promoting your services and engaging with potential clients.

Examples:
- Hootsuite: Manage multiple social media accounts and schedule posts.
- Buffer: Schedule posts and track social media performance.

5. Client Communication Tools

a. Email Management: For professional communication and client outreach.

Examples:
- Gmail: Popular email service with robust features.
- Outlook: Comprehensive email and calendar management tool.

b. Video Conferencing Tools: For virtual consultations and meetings with clients.
   Examples:
   - Zoom: Video conferencing with screen sharing and meeting recording.
   - Microsoft Teams: Collaboration tool with video conferencing features.
   - Google Meet: Secure video meetings with integration into Google Workspace.

c. Messaging and Collaboration Tools: For team communication and collaboration.
   Examples:
   - Slack: Team communication and collaboration platform.
   - Microsoft Teams: Integrated communication and collaboration tool.

6. **Legal and Compliance Tools**
   a. Business Insurance: To protect against liabilities and potential damages.
      Examples:
      - General liability insurance
      - Professional liability insurance
   b. Licensing and Permits: Ensure compliance with local regulations and obtain necessary licenses.
      Examples:
      - Business license
      - Permits specific to your location

c. **Copyright and Usage Agreements:** To protect your intellectual property and set terms for content usage.
     Examples:
     - Standard copyright agreements
     - Usage rights agreements

7. **Professional Development**
   a. **Training and Workshops:** For improving editing skills and staying updated with industry trends.
   Examples:
     - Online courses (e.g., Udemy, Coursera)
     - Editing and proofreading workshops and webinars
   b. **Networking:** For connecting with other professionals and potential clients.
      Examples:
      - Editing communities and forums
      - Industry conferences and meetups

By investing in these tools and resources, you'll be well-equipped to start and run a successful copyediting and proofreading business. Focus on delivering high-quality editing services, maintaining strong client relationships, and continuously improving your skills to build and sustain your business.

44. Resume Writing

Resume writing services help job seekers create professional resumes and cover letters that stand out to employers. Entrepreneurs with HR or recruitment experience can offer personalized consultations, resume writing, and LinkedIn profile optimization services, helping clients advance their careers.

Starting a resume writing business involves a mix of specialized tools to help you create professional resumes, manage client interactions, and handle business operations. Here's a list of tools and resources you'll need to launch and run a successful resume writing business:

3 Key Things to Start this type of Business:

1. **Editing Tools & Software**: Invest in specialized editing tools such as **Grammarly**, **ProWritingAid**, or **Hemingway Editor** to enhance your efficiency. These tools help you catch grammar errors, improve sentence structure, and ensure style consistency. For formatting manuscripts or documents, programs like **Microsoft Word** with Track Changes enabled or **Google Docs** are essential for real-time collaboration with clients.

2. **Attention to Detail & Style Guides**: Develop a deep knowledge of style guides such as **The Chicago Manual of Style**, **AP Stylebook**, or **MLA**, depending on your

target market (academic, publishing, business). These style guides ensure consistency and accuracy in your proofreading and copyediting work, helping you deliver professional and polished results.
3. **Portfolio & Client Outreach**: Create a portfolio by offering free or discounted services at the start to build a reputation. Showcase your ability to enhance clarity, grammar, and flow in written work. Additionally, establish an online presence—via a professional website or LinkedIn profile—to attract clients from various industries, including authors, businesses, and publishers.

To make your copyediting and proofreading business a success, marketing is essential. Here are a few strategies that can help you grow and attract clients:

1. Build a Strong Online Presence
- **Website**: Create a professional website showcasing your services, portfolio, client testimonials, and pricing packages. Make it easy for potential clients to contact you.
- **Social Media**: Use platforms like LinkedIn, Twitter, and Instagram to network with authors, businesses, and publishers. Share tips on grammar, editing, or writing trends to position yourself as an expert.
- **SEO Optimization**: Optimize your website and content with relevant keywords (e.g.,

"copyediting services," "proofreading for authors") to improve search engine visibility.

2. **Networking & Referrals**
   - **Reach Out to Authors and Publishers**: Build relationships with indie authors, publishers, and content creators through direct outreach or participation in online forums, webinars, and writing groups. Referrals from satisfied clients can help spread the word about your business.
   - **Join Freelance Platforms**: Sign up on platforms like **Upwork**, **Fiverr**, or **Reedsy**, where clients are actively looking for editing services. These platforms can help you build a client base quickly.

3. **Offer Special Packages or Niches**
   - **Tailor Services for Specific Markets**: Offer packages for different client needs—e.g., manuscript evaluation for authors, content editing for businesses, or academic proofreading for students. Specializing in a niche (e.g., self-published authors, academic papers) can give you a competitive edge.
   - **Provide Free Resources**: Offer free downloadable guides, such as a "Self-Editing Checklist" or grammar tips, to attract leads and build trust with potential clients.

Combining a solid online presence, networking, and specialized services can significantly increase the chances of success for your copyediting and proofreading business

By investing in these tools and resources, you'll be well-equipped to start and manage a successful resume writing business. Focus on providing high-quality, customized resumes, maintaining strong client relationships, and continuously improving your skills to build and grow your business.

45. Virtual Assistant

Virtual assistant services provide administrative and operational support to businesses and entrepreneurs remotely. Entrepreneurs with organizational and multitasking skills can offer scheduling, email management, and research assistance services, helping clients streamline their workflows and focus on core tasks.

Starting a virtual assistant (VA) business involves equipping yourself with a variety of tools to manage tasks, communicate with clients, and handle administrative work efficiently.

By utilizing these tools and resources, you'll be well-prepared to start and manage a successful virtual assistant business. Focus on delivering high-quality services, maintaining strong client relationships, and continuously improving your skills to build and grow your business. Here are 5 key things to get started:

1. **Reliable Equipment & Workspace**
   - **Computer & High-Speed Internet**: A fast, reliable computer and internet connection are essential for handling various tasks like scheduling, communication, and document management.
   - **Dedicated Workspace**: A quiet, organized workspace enhances productivity and professionalism during virtual meetings or client calls.

2. **Task Management & Communication Tools**
   - **Project Management Software**: Use tools like **Trello**, **Asana**, or **ClickUp** to manage client projects, track tasks, and stay organized.
   - **Communication Tools**: **Slack**, **Zoom**, or **Skype** are key for interacting with clients, providing updates, and holding virtual meetings. Email management is also critical for organizing client communications.
3. **Payment & Time Tracking Software**
   - **Time Tracking Tools**: Use tools like **Toggl** or **Harvest** to track billable hours, ensuring accurate invoicing for clients.
   - **Invoicing Software**: Use platforms like **QuickBooks** or **PayPal** to send invoices, manage payments, and track your income.
4. **Niche & Specialized Services**
   - Decide on your niche or specialization. Will you focus on **email management, customer support, social media scheduling**, or **research**? Having a clear focus helps you attract the right clients.
   - Build expertise in specific industries, like e-commerce, real estate, or coaching, to stand out and offer tailored services.
5. **Portfolio & Client Testimonials**
   - Build a portfolio that showcases your skills in **administrative work, task management**, or **social media assistance**. Include case

studies or testimonials from past clients to build credibility.
- You can offer a few discounted or free services initially to gather testimonials, then transition to paid services.

How to Market Your Virtual Assistant Business:
1. **Leverage Freelance Platforms**
     - **Upwork** and **Fiverr** are excellent places to market your services. Optimize your profile with clear, specific offerings, showcase your expertise, and regularly apply to relevant job postings.
     - **LinkedIn**: Use LinkedIn to connect with potential clients, participate in industry groups, and share helpful content related to virtual assistance. A strong LinkedIn profile can attract clients organically.
2. **Create a Website & Social Media Presence**
     - Build a professional website where you list your services, portfolio, pricing, and contact information. Incorporate **SEO strategies** to attract organic traffic from clients searching for VA services.
     - Use social media platforms like **Facebook** and **Instagram** to market your services. Share productivity tips, testimonials, and examples of work to engage potential clients.

3. **Networking & Cold Outreach**
    - Join virtual assistant and small business networking groups online (on platforms like **Facebook** or **Reddit**) to connect with entrepreneurs needing help.
    - Engage in **cold emailing** or **LinkedIn messaging** to reach out to potential clients in your target industry, introducing your services and how you can help streamline their operations.

46. Life Coaching

Life coaching services empower individuals to set and achieve personal and professional goals, overcome obstacles, and improve their overall well-being. Entrepreneurs with coaching certifications and counseling skills can offer one-on-one sessions, workshops, and accountability programs, helping clients unlock their full potential.

Starting a life coaching business involves a combination of tools to facilitate coaching sessions, manage client relationships, and run your business efficiently.

1. **Video Conferencing Software**
   - **Zoom**, **Skype**, or **Google Meet**: These platforms allow you to conduct virtual coaching sessions with clients. Video calls are essential for life coaches working with clients remotely, providing a personal and engaging experience.
2. **Scheduling & Calendar Tools**
   - **Acuity Scheduling**, **Calendly**, or **Google Calendar**: These tools enable clients to book coaching sessions directly, sync with your calendar, and help avoid scheduling conflicts. Automated scheduling tools save time and provide a seamless experience for both you and your clients.
3. **Client Management System (CRM)**
   - **Dubsado**, **HoneyBook**, or **CoachAccountable**: These platforms help

you manage client data, track progress, and handle invoicing, contracts, and follow-ups. A CRM keeps all your client information organized and ensures smooth communication.

4. Goal Tracking & Progress Monitoring Tools

- **Trello**, **Asana**, or **CoachAccountable**: Use these tools to help clients set goals, track progress, and monitor their achievements. Visual goal tracking boosts client accountability and allows you to provide clear feedback on their development.

5. Coaching Certification & Resource Materials

- **Accreditation**: If you're not already certified, earning a certification from a recognized organization like the **International Coach Federation (ICF)** or **Certified Life Coach Institute** is critical. This not only boosts credibility but gives you access to valuable coaching resources and ongoing professional development materials.
- **Worksheets and Coaching Templates**: Tools like **Google Docs** or pre-made coaching templates help structure sessions and give clients clear action steps. Use these to provide personalized coaching materials for clients.

Additional Tips for Running a Successful Life Coaching Business:

- **Marketing Strategy**: Build a professional website and use social media platforms

(LinkedIn, Instagram) to promote your services, offer free webinars, or share motivational content.
- **Payment & Invoicing Tools**: Use platforms like **PayPal**, **Stripe**, or **QuickBooks** to handle client payments and invoicing seamlessly.

6. Confidentiality Agreements & Legal Contracts

Having well-structured confidentiality agreements not only ensures client privacy but also enhances your professionalism and credibility as a life coach. This builds trust with clients, allowing them to feel safe and open during sessions.

- **Digital Signature Tools**: Use platforms like **DocuSign** or **HelloSign** to send and receive signed confidentiality agreements and coaching contracts. These ensure that sensitive information shared during coaching sessions remains private and protected.
- **Legal Templates**: You can either draft your own confidentiality agreements or use templates from services like **LegalZoom** or **Rocket Lawyer**. It's essential to have agreements that clearly define what information will remain confidential and outline the terms of your coaching relationship.

By leveraging these tools to begin, you'll set a strong foundation for running a smooth and professional life coaching business. The key is to start with the right systems in place to manage administrative tasks efficiently, allowing you to focus on what matters most—helping clients achieve their goals. However, the true success of your business will come from continuously working at it. As you gain more experience, refine your processes, and build client relationships, your business will evolve.

Consistency is crucial. By regularly reviewing and improving your client management, communication, and goal-tracking systems, you'll not only enhance the client experience but also improve your ability to scale. Your goal should always be to keep progressing, both as a coach and as a business owner, so that you're constantly delivering value and empowering your clients to unlock their full potential. With dedication and a commitment to growth, your business will flourish over time.

Inspirational Stories

Wally Blume - Founder of Denali Flavors

Wally Blume spent most of his career in the dairy industry, working for various ice cream companies. As he approached retirement age in his late 50s, instead of slowing down, he decided to start his own business.

In 1995, at the age of 57, Blume founded Denali Flavors with his wife June. They started by creating unique ice cream flavors in their home kitchen. Their breakthrough came when they developed "Moose Tracks," a vanilla ice cream with peanut butter cups and fudge swirl.

Blume leveraged his industry connections to license the flavor to regional dairies. The flavor was a hit, and Denali Flavors grew rapidly. By the time Blume was in his 70s, Moose Tracks had become one of the top-selling ice cream flavors in the U.S.

Today, Denali Flavors generates over $80 million in annual revenues. Blume's story shows how decades of industry experience can be turned into a successful business venture in later life.

Gail Dunn - Founder of Gail's Personalized Gifts

Gail Dunn worked as a public school teacher for 30 years. As she neared retirement, she wanted to supplement her pension and pursue a long-held interest in crafting.

At age 58, just two years before her planned retirement from teaching, Dunn started selling personalized gifts on Etsy. She began with a small investment, using her crafting skills to create custom wedding hangers, bridesmaid gifts, and other personalized items.

Dunn worked on her business in the evenings and weekends while still teaching. By the time she retired from teaching at 60, her Etsy shop was generating enough income to match her previous salary.

In the years since, Gail's Personalized Gifts has continued to grow. Dunn has expanded her product line, hired part-time help, and even opened a small brick-and-mortar store in her hometown. Her business now generates over $250,000 in annual revenue.

Dunn's success demonstrates how turning a hobby into a business can provide both financial security and personal fulfillment in retirement. Her story is particularly inspiring as it shows how digital platforms like Etsy can help retirees start businesses with minimal upfront investment.

Your Next Step: Turning Ideas into Reality

Well, my friend, we've reached the end of Retirement Ready: 40+ Low-Budget Business Ideas for Financial Independence. But really, this is just the beginning—your beginning.

Remember when you first picked up this book? Maybe you were looking for ways to supplement your retirement income, or perhaps you wanted to reignite a passion you've always had but never had the time to pursue. Whatever brought you here, I hope you're now filled with excitement and new ideas for this next chapter of life.

We've explored over 40 different business ideas that require little investment. From freelance consulting to pet sitting, online tutoring to other online options—there's something here for everyone. The best part? You don't need to dip heavily into your retirement savings to get started. All you need is creativity, determination, and a willingness to try something new.

I can imagine you might be wondering, "This all sounds great, but where do I start?" Well, ask yourself this: which idea resonated with you the most? Which one had you thinking, "I could do that!" That's your starting point.

Pick one idea. Just one. Don't worry about choosing the "perfect" idea—there's no such thing.

The beauty of these low-cost ventures is that you can always pivot if something isn't working. The important thing is to start.

Once you've made your choice, it's time to take that first step. Whether it's setting up a website or making your first product, do it today. Not tomorrow, not next week—today. Even if it's just a small step, it's progress.

If you already have a hobby you enjoy, why not turn that into a business? For example, if you love crafting or collecting vintage items, consider opening an Etsy shop. You'll be able to sell your creations or finds to a global market, all while doing something you love. In retirement, this can be a fulfilling way to spend your time and make extra income.

Remember, every successful entrepreneur started exactly where you are now—with an idea and the decision to act on it.

As you embark on this journey, keep these tips in mind:

1. Leverage your experience: Your skills, knowledge, and connections are your most valuable assets.
2. Embrace technology: There are plenty of free or low-cost digital tools available to help you run your business.

3. Start small, dream big: Begin with a manageable goal, but keep your long-term vision in sight.
4. Adapt as needed: The business world evolves quickly, and your flexibility is key to staying relevant.
5. Continue learning: Each challenge is an opportunity to grow and improve.
6. Network with others: Connect with fellow entrepreneurs in your community or online—they can provide support and advice.
7. Focus on value: Satisfied customers are the foundation of any successful business.

There will be highs and lows—that's all part of the entrepreneurial adventure. Embrace the journey, learn from the challenges, and above all, enjoy the process.

Financial freedom isn't just about money. It's about living life on your terms. It's about waking up every day excited to do something that's truly yours. So, are you ready to take the first step toward a fulfilling retirement business? To turn your dreams into a reality?

The road ahead is clear, and the opportunities are endless. All you need to do is choose your path and start walking. And if you stumble along the way, don't worry—that's part of the journey too. Pick yourself up, dust yourself off, and keep moving forward.

Your retirement can be the beginning of something extraordinary. So set your goals, make a plan, and start today. Your future self will thank you.

Now go out there and make it happen! I'm rooting for you.

www.ingramcontent.com/pod-product-compliance
Lightning Source LLC
Chambersburg PA
CBHW071051240526
45471CB00015B/1559